Editor-in-Chief and Founder:
   Lyndon H. LaRouche, Jr.
Editorial Board: *Lyndon H. LaRouche, Jr. , Helga Zepp-LaRouche, Robert Ingraham, Tony Papert, Gerald Rose, Dennis Small, Jeffrey Steinberg, William Wertz*
Co-Editors: *Robert Ingraham, Tony Papert*
Managing Editor: *Nancy Spannaus*
Technology: *Marsha Freeman*
Books: *Katherine Notley*
Ebooks: *Richard Burden*
Graphics: *Alan Yue*
Photos: *Stuart Lewis*
Circulation Manager: *Stanley Ezrol*

INTELLIGENCE DIRECTORS
Counterintelligence: *Jeffrey Steinberg, Michele Steinberg*
Economics: *John Hoefle, Marcia Merry Baker, Paul Gallagher*
History: *Anton Chaitkin*
Ibero-America: *Dennis Small*
Russia and Eastern Europe: *Rachel Douglas*
United States: *Debra Freeman*

INTERNATIONAL BUREAUS
Bogotá: *Miriam Redondo*
Berlin: *Rainer Apel*
Copenhagen: *Tom Gillesberg*
Houston: *Harley Schlanger*
Lima: *Sara Madueño*
Melbourne: *Robert Barwick*
Mexico City: *Gerardo Castilleja Chávez*
New Delhi: *Ramtanu Maitra*
Paris: *Christine Bierre*
Stockholm: *Ulf Sandmark*
United Nations, N.Y.C.: *Leni Rubinstein*
Washington, D.C.: *William Jones*
Wiesbaden: *Göran Haglund*

ON THE WEB
e-mail: eirns@larouchepub.com
www.larouchepub.com
www.executiveintelligencereview.com
www.larouchepub.com/eiw
Webmaster: *John Sigerson*
Assistant Webmaster: *George Hollis*
Editor, Arabic-language edition: *Hussein Askary*

EIR (ISSN 0273-6314) *is published weekly (50 issues), by EIR News Service, Inc., P.O. Box 17390, Washington, D.C. 20041-0390. (703) 777-9451 ext. 415*

European Headquarters: E.I.R. GmbH, Postfach Bahnstrasse 9a, D-65205, Wiesbaden, Germany
Tel: 49-611-73650
Homepage: http://www.eirna.com
e-mail: eirna@eirna.com
Director: Georg Neudecker

Montreal, Canada: 514-461-1557

Denmark: EIR - Danmark, Sankt Knuds Vej 11, basement left, DK-1903 Frederiksberg, Denmark. Tel.: +45 35 43 60 40, Fax: +45 35 43 87 57. e-mail: eirdk@hotmail.com.

Mexico City: EIR, Sor Juana Inés de la Cruz 242-2 Col. Agricultura C.P. 11360 Delegación M. Hidalgo, México D.F. Tel. (5525) 5318-2301 eirmexico@gmail.com

Canada Post Publication Sales Agreement #40683579

Postmaster: Send all address changes to *EIR*, P.O. Box 17390, Washington, D.C. 20041-0390.

Signed articles in *EIR* represent the views of the authors, and not necessarily those of the Editorial Board.

World History Enters A New Epoch

A Different Quality of Thinking

Below are edited excerpts of the Sept. 12 LaRouche PAC Policy Committee *discussion of its 9/11 Weekend "Living Memorial" Events in the New York area.*

Diane Sare: Good afternoon, and welcome to the weekly LaRouche PAC Policy Committee discussion. I am Diane Sare; Matt Ogden is not with us today, and we are filming from the Manhattan Project. We have here in our studio Mike Steger from San Francisco; Kesha Rogers, from Houston, Texas; Bill Roberts from Detroit, Michigan, and sometimes Manhattan; and joining us over Google Hangouts, live, Dave Christie, from Seattle, Washington; and Rachel Brinkley, back in Boston, Massachusetts, although she's been here with us for a number of days.

And I can just say that the occasion that brings us together is that this weekend has been the fifteenth anniversary of the most hideous terrorist attacks on our nation, which were particularly hard-felt in Manhattan with the attacks on the World Trade Center in New York City and the Pentagon on Sept. 11, 2001. And as our viewers know, Mr. LaRouche has made a very strong point that we have yet to secure justice in that case, where you had close to 3,000 Americans murdered on that day, and thousands more have died in wars based on lies in the so-called "War on Terror," not to mention millions of people who have been killed and displaced globally as a result of these wars.

And what we've experienced over these days thus far, with so far three performances of the Mozart *Requiem* which were sponsored by the Foundation for the Revival of Classical Culture and which the Schiller Institute Community Chorus participated in, is, I think, a great potential for the transformation of the United States which is urgently important at this time, as we are on the brink of the biggest blowout of the trans-Atlantic financial system that anyone can imagine, as well as being on the brink of a Renaissance greater than anyone can imagine, developing from the new paradigm as led by leaders like Presidents Putin of Russia and Xi Jinping of China.

I will not say more, but open the discussion here for people who have been a part of this process in other spots.

Michael Steger: Well, I can say, coming in from San Francisco and only getting a sense of just the concerts,— but I think the process building up into it was also fairly substantial. And as Lyn [LaRouche] said, the people who would be most touched would be the people who were brought into the process of the choruses and the whole idea of making an intervention into the culture around the concerts. But you have to say, there were over 1,100 people in a Manhattan church on Saturday.

There were events happening under other auspices, and the reports we got were that they were far less substantial and thoughtful. But what really is the meaning of this process? For the chorus's 80-100 plus people on Saturday and on Sunday?

And I thought what was probably most touching to me: one of the firefighters of the Sunday Mass,— we participated at the Co-Cathedral of St. Joseph in Brooklyn. They do a Mass every year for the firefighters. There were twenty-four of them from this battalion that gave their lives in the Towers. And so they had one of the leaders of that battalion speaking in honor of them, and saying that we will never forget what they did. You heard the overtones of the Gettysburg Address. And it was very emotional. There weren't very many dry eyes in the house, including the chorus and orchestra and everybody else participating,— let alone the families of the fallen. They brought in flags representing each of their firefighters that fell on that day. As we discussed earlier, these people were *murdered*; this was a murder against the American people *en masse*.

But once these remarks were done, and our chorus was brought forward to sing,— you have the whole orchestra, the whole performance, and John Sigerson, our conductor, had to make a decision: Are we going to continue that intense emotion of the memory of these people who had fallen, or are we going to try to elevate it now, through Mozart, towards an even higher domain?— something of an optimism toward the future, a triumph in a sense. And I thought the performance yesterday, although it had a few kinks, really captured that quality; they had the quality of timing the way John approached it, and the connection that the whole orchestra and chorus had to the proceedings. It was very touching.

But you saw it go from looking back on the last fifteen years, to looking forward to the next one hundred years. That was that quality that we captured with the musical performance....

Rachel Brinkley: It is a new paradigm. People in the United States,— frankly, no one understands what's happening in the world. There's not really a single American for the most part, who really has any idea what's happening, that there's a different quality of thinking. And what happened at these events, especially on Sunday,— it was that quality of thinking brought to the United States.

And especially with the discussion with the firefighters—there was discussion of what were these firefighters doing, rushing—when everyone else was rushing to their safety, looking out for their safety, what is it in a firefighter that makes them *enter* the danger and put their lives at risk? And these twenty-four firefighters lost their lives for that principle, for this profound principle which goes against what most people would think about their own identity, preserving their own safety.

But that is the quality of the new paradigm, this idea, and this was also what was brought out in the Mozart *Requiem* music, a parallel idea. And this is also what President Xi spoke about at the G-20 conference, when he said that he was most proud of lifting the world out of poverty. That was the discussion. He said, we've lifted 700 million people out of poverty; we want to end global poverty—that's our next step.

So this is not a self-interest motivation. This is a different quality of thinking of looking at mankind in general, as a whole. As those firefighters were thinking, as they rushed into the building, they weren't worried about who it was they were going to save: They were going to save everyone in that building, and I think that's the quality that is the new paradigm.

EIR Contents

www.larouchepub.com Volume 43, Number 38, September 16, 2016

Cover This Week

Hangzhou West Lake

CC/Cliff Subagio

I. The September Summits

The G-20 Summit: 'A Change of World-Historic Dimensions'

Here are excerpts from Helga Zepp-LaRouche's remarks to the LaRouche PAC Webcast of Sept. 9, 2016.

Host Jason Ross: Let's bring on Helga Zepp-La-Rouche now. Helga was a participant in the T-20 meeting, which was a meeting with think tanks, a "Think-20" meeting held in China in preparation for the G-20 heads of state summit which just occurred. Helga, let me ask you about this. In your view, how have these events over the past couple of weeks changed the world?

Helga Zepp-LaRouche: Well, I think it is a change of world-historic dimensions, because what has occurred as a result of the Vladivostok Eastern Economic Forum, the G-20, and then the ASEAN conference, is a tremendous change in where the power center of the world is. Just Let me very quickly go through what the significance each of these of these different conferences is.

The summit in Vladivostok signified the integration of the Eurasian Economic Union with the Silk Road/Belt and Road initiative of China. That is very impor-

kremlin.ru

Russian President Vladimir Putin speaking at the plenary session of the Sept. 2-3 Eastern Economic Forum in Vladivostok, Russia, with featured guests, seated right to left: Japan Prime Minister Shinzo Abe and South Korean President Park Geun-hye.

tant because Prime Minister Abe of Japan and President Park of South Korea also participated, and there were agreements on long-term investments in development of the Far East of Russia, of Siberia, of huge energy investments, and the integration of all of these economies of Asia.

This was followed by the G-20 Summit, which I think was really an absolute breakthrough. First of all, China had put an enormous amount of effort into its preparation, by convening many, many pre-conferences, starting a year ago, on many, many levels: ministers, think-tanks, institutions, and organizations. The intention of China was to transform the G-20 from a mechanism which only responds to crises like 2008— the financial crash of Lehman Brothers—into an organization which would form an alliance of countries to form a global governance mechanism which is problem-solving. Xi Jinping said repeatedly he wants to transform the G-20 from a "talk shop," into a group of nations which *act* together. This was accomplished in many ways.

The Western media are hysterically and desperately trying to belittle this outcome of the conference by saying that there were all of these "issues," but the only people who raised these so-called "issues," like the South China Sea conflict, the issue of the Arbitration Court in The Hague, and all other divisive issues,— was really the Western nations.

In reality, what happened is that the overwhelming number of nations are moving to adopt the Chinese model of economy. They are very right to do so, because China has proven to be an economic miracle of such dimensions, as Xi Jinping said, as to have transformed a country of 1.4 billion people that has never before been undertaken in history on that scale,— and the fact that China could uplift 700 million people out of poverty into a very decent living standard, is also unprecedented. One of the outcomes of the summit was the adoption of a plan to eliminate poverty all over China by 2020, that is, only four years from now.

China succeeded in putting the Chinese economic model on the agenda as the attractive model for everybody to join, in a "win-win" perspective. Many countries are saying, "Yes, we can have the same economic development as China; that is much more desirable, than joining the United States, or NATO, or the Europeans in geopolitical confrontation."

The success of this summit is really unbelievable. It has changed the situation in the world, I think for the better, because the unipolar world definitely does not exist any more. As a matter of fact, *Forbes* magazine and *Time* magazine had quite hysterical articles saying that Obama's "Asia pivot" policy has completely failed. This was the last opportunity to woo the countries of the region, but this completely failed, and the "Asia pivot" of Obama is completely dead; it failed.

The G-77 [developing countries], the Non-Aligned Movement, the ASEAN countries — they are all are now moving in a completely different direction, and especially the fact that South Korea and Japan participated with Russia and China in this Vladivostok conference, proves that these countries, which are obviously allied with the United States, nevertheless do not want confrontation against Russia and China any longer.

So this is extremely important. And it means primarily that those countries of the world which are not of the old regime of the World Bank, the IMF—the so-called "Washington Consensus," the so-called Bretton Woods institutions—they had no voice, and they now have a voice.

I think it is really very important that China explicitly adopted developing nations and emerging economies. First of all, they invited a very large representation of them to participate in the G-20 summit. China expressed the absolute commitment that every fruit of technological innovation would be shared with these countries, in order not to hold up their development. Now, this is a beautiful idea, which was first expressed by the German thinker Nicholas of Cusa in the 15th Century, who already then had said that science and technology are so important for the development of mankind, that every time there is a new invention, it should be put in an international pool—to use modern words—and that every country should have access to it, so as not to be slowed down in their development.

It's an incredible change, because it means that, for the first time, an idea has been realized which was expressed by my husband Lyndon LaRouche in 1975, when he proposed a plan to develop the Third World, and he called it the International Development Bank (IDB). This was the idea which he presented both in Bonn, Germany at the time, and in Milan. He wanted at that time to have a $400 billion transfer of technology per year to the developing sector from the advanced countries, in order to build up infrastructure, and build up industrialization and agriculture in the Third World.

He gave a very concrete form to a demand of the Non-Aligned Movement, which in 1976 at the Non-

Aligned Movement in Colombo, Sri Lanka, had adopted a resolution demanding a just New World Economic Order. In that Non-Aligned Movement resolution, 90% of the wording was the same as that of the IDB. But what then happened was that all the leaders of the countries who had lead the initiative to fight for this—like Mrs. Gandhi from India, Mrs. Bandaranaike from Sri Lanka, Z.A. Bhutto from Pakistan—all these leaders were either killed or destabilized; and this whole effort had a tremendous setback, and as a result, it did not succeed.

Now as some of our viewers may know, we have been fighting in the LaRouche Movement ever since that time—it's now 40 years we have been fighting for the realization of the IDB or an IDB-like plan for the Third World, but the World Bank and the IMF, for all these years have done the exact opposite. The IMF conditionalities completely prevent any kind of development, by forcing developing countries to pay debt instead of investing in infrastructure. They even created the debt trap, to make it impossible for countries to develop. So, the miserable condition of Africa, and many other countries in Asia and the Middle East and some countries in South America, is the result of the conscious policy of suppressing development.

Now, after the Asia crisis [in 1997-98], the Asian countries obviously realized that they had to do something to protect themselves against attacks such as the speculation of George Soros at the time, so a process of creating new institutions developed. One was the Chiang Mai Initiative. But then recently—about three years ago—China took the leadership together with other BRICS countries, to create a completely alternative set of banking institutions:

- The Asian Infrastructure Investment Bank (AIIB)
- The New Development Bank of the BRICS
- The New Silk Road Fund
- The Maritime Silk Road Fund
- The Shanghai Cooperation Organization Bank.

aiib.org

President Xi Jinping and heads of delegations representing the 57 prospective founding member nations of the Asian Infrastructure Investment Bank in Beijing, June 29, 2015, following the signing ceremony of the Articles of Agreement.

So, you now have a completely alternate system of banking which is *not* a casino, but only grants credit for investment in real infrastructure in the real economy.

So, what is happening now? I think people have to appreciate this, that what happened at the G-20 meeting is the victory of a struggle of 40 years at least, to make it possible for human beings in Africa, in the so-called developing sector, to have a chance for the future. Such a powerful coalition has now emerged—the strategic alliance between China and Russia. Putin was the guest of honor at this G-20 meeting—so the world really has changed. It's very important to say that these articles in *Forbes* magazine and *Time* magazine really don't get it. It's not anti-American; it's not anti-European. Xi Jinping and the other leaders have expressed many times that they want the United States and Europe to join in a "win-win" perspective.

So what is on the table now as a result of the G-20 meeting, is for the first time a strategic initiative which is not geopolitical, because it offers a level of reason on which to cooperate internationally for the common aims of mankind. I think this is a tremendous historical breakthrough, and we really must make sure that the American people find out what it is, and not be misled by mediocre journalists, who can only think in geopolitical terms. It's like somebody who is evil, cannot

Chinese President Xi Jinping presiding over the opening ceremony at the G-20 Summit in Hangzhou, China, Sept. 4, 2016.

Xinhua/Li Xueren

imagine, when he is talking to a really good person, that the other person is not also evil. So what you read in the Western media is just the projection of the degenerate thinking of the media. But that is not what happened at this summit. So, let's make sure people really understand the historic significance of this change.

Ross: Great! I think what you went through in terms of the history of your involvement, of your husband Lyndon LaRouche's involvement, of the LaRouche Movement's involvement over the past four decades in creating the victory for the policy that's being announced at these conferences, really goes to show the power of an idea: That over cynicism or over what seemed to be the structures and control of things, a good idea and successful and intense and ongoing organizing for it, really can make things happen.

I was going to ask if you wanted to say more about the history of the LaRouche Movement's involvement in this; or also if you have anything to say about how we're going to get the United States to join in this development instead of being opposed to it?

Zepp-LaRouche: Well, first of all, I would like to make a short comment on the ASEAN conference, because that followed the G-20 meeting; and that dispute is now settled. Because the ASEAN countries together with China, all agreed that all the disputes will be solved

through peaceful negotiation and dialogue; they will work out a Code of Conduct by the middle of next year to this effect, and jointly fight threats to security like terrorism and other threats. They will act on the basis of the UN Convention of the Law of the Sea, or UNCLOS; and that means all these efforts to hype up the conflict between the Philippines and China with The Hague Arbitration Court, have not succeeded. This was an effort to cause disunity, but this ASEAN conference said, "No, we want to have joint economic development. We will revive the regional economic development organization."

So, it shows that the foreign policy of China—not only at the G-20—changed the agenda completely. But also in terms of regional conflict, that if you have a "win-win" perspective where you take into account the interests of the other, you can find solutions.

So then what is left for Obama, some papers said, was the implementation of the TPP; but as you already mentioned, both the House and the Senate and the two Presidential candidates all have said the TPP is out. The leaders of the two Houses have said it will not get onto the agenda this year, which means not during the time of Obama. So, the TPP is dead; and the TTIP—it's the European version of the same thing—is also dead. So, I think the world really has changed. Unipolar demands and the idea that one country can decide what the rules are for another country are no longer workable. We have entered a completely new era of respect for the sovereignty of the other country, and an alliance, essentially of republics, for a greater good.

This is obviously a really important development. Not only does it mean that the United States has the chance to go back to the foreign policy of John Quincy Adams—because that is exactly what he had outlined for the United States to do. But it also means that the kind of system of perfectly sovereign nation-states working together for a joint development—which we especially have pushed—naturally Mr. LaRouche has pushed, for over 50 years—that this is now becoming a reality.

So, I think that we can be very happy about that, because the LaRouche Movement for the last 40 years, but especially the last 25 years, convened literally hundreds of conferences around the world, in every major U.S. and European city, in Rio de Janeiro, in Sao Paolo, Brasilia, Mexico, Beijing, New Delhi, Moscow. We also Many held many conferences and seminars in Australia, in Egypt, and in other African countries. I think we now have a renaissance movement and a world movement for development.

Since you mentioned the beautiful gala concert which preceded the G-20, this was, in a certain sense, similar to what we are doing with the dialogue of Classical culture. The G-20 summit started with a very beautiful series of Chinese folk songs, then it had scenes from the ballet *Swan Lake*—danced in a lake—so the dancers would make a kind of little fountain with each step, because they were stepping into the water. It gave it an unbelievable effect. And naturally, the fact that they chose the *Ode to Joy*, the beautiful poem by Schiller composed by Beethoven, where the text at one point says, "All men become brothers," *"Alle Menschen werden Brüder,"* which is the poetical expression of the "win-win" perspective, that there is a higher goal of mankind. And the fact that they chose that to be the high point of the gala, really shows that they have understood something very fundamental. They said, "Text written by Friedrich Schiller" so naturally many people would have thought about the Schiller Institute. We have used the *Ode to Joy* many times to express the same idea.

So, I think that we can be really proud, because we did not do everything, but we had a very good role in producing this beautiful result.

Ross: Helga, let's paint for our viewers an idea of a future, if we could. With the United States dropping this zero-sum game geopolitical approach, with the United States and Europe adopting the proposals that you're putting forward, what could the world be like in five or ten years? Is this an endless, perpetual fight? Or what does victory look like? What could the world be like?

Zepp-LaRouche: Well, I think things can change very quickly if the United States and Europe adopt the Glass-Steagall banking separation law, which is, as you know, in bills in Congress and the Senate. I was very happy when I saw that "Black Lives Matter" is now demanding from Hillary Clinton that she should adopt Glass-Steagall. Because you can only fight racism if you fight the injustice caused by Wall Street. I thought this was an irony. So, let me say something briefly about the bankruptcy of the United States and Europe.

China has growth rates anywhere from 6% to 7%, they want to have now 7% again; India has even had 8% growth rates. Other Asian countries are going in the same direction. And what is the growth rate in Europe? The new (GDP) statistics of the Eurozone just came out—0.3%; and in France, Italy, and Finland—0%. Naturally, all the parameters are really alarming. The headlines today are that Draghi, the head of the European Central Bank, has no more options. He's running out of options because of negative interest rates, quantitative easing, and helicopter money. All of these are signs of a dying system. And then naturally, you have Deutsche Bank, which has all the same parameters as Lehman Brothers in 2008—the credit default swap costs are now exactly those for Lehman Brothers just before it blew up. If that happens, you could have the next 2008 crisis this September or October.

So, the fight for Glass-Steagall is super-urgent; and naturally, as Lyndon LaRouche has stressed very emphatically with his Four Laws, this is not enough. Then you need to have a credit system, and you need to issue credit for real investment.

Now, if these changes can be done quickly—this year—even before the U.S. election occurs, then there is no reason why the world cannot enter a completely New Paradigm which would stop geopolitical confrontation. The danger of war is not yet eliminated. I don't want to pretend there's security when it's not there. But at least with the new alliance between Russia, Turkey, and Iran, the Syria question can be solved. With the "28 pages" and the JASTA bill, maybe the Saudi support for terrorism can also be brought to an end. Then, even the German Economic Development Minister from the CSU—the Christian Social Union—made a speech yesterday in the Parliament, demanding a Marshall Plan for Africa. He said, this present global system is a failure. It has created forms of early capitalism in many parts of the world. This cannot continue. In the next 30 years, two billion babies will be born in Africa alone. They will need many jobs, many teachers, and real investment. He demanded that the WTO [World Trade Organization] be transformed from a free trade into a

German Development Minister Gerd Müller.

fair trade mechanism. So, this is a conservative politician from Germany, of the Merkel government; and he's the only one who so far has the courage and the vision to say these things. But what he said is actually true.

With the new alliance I described earlier in the context of the G-20, now Japan is starting to invest massively in Africa, and this was welcomed by China. China said we are not in Africa for competitive reasons, but the need for development is so big, that we are happy if India and Japan are all investing. And naturally, Europe should invest. The United States should build up the Middle East and overcome poverty there: rebuild the war-torn region—Iraq, Afghanistan, Syria, Yemen, Libya, all of Africa. If all of these countries were developed with the extension of the New Silk Road program, and all countries would work together, poverty could be eliminated in a very short period of time, maybe in two years.

Gerd Müller, the German Development Minister, pointed out that 80% of Africans still do not have access to electricity. Now that could be very, very quickly changed. We have developed in our program of the World Land-Bridge, a comprehensive development plan for Africa. Infrastructure, bridges, ports, fast train systems, roads, the development of agriculture and industry, the creation of large amounts of freshwater to fight the desert through peaceful nuclear energy, desalination of ocean water, and the ionization of moisture in the atmosphere. In a few years, Africa and those parts of the world which are still in poverty, could look like

beautiful gardens, with forests, agriculture, and new cities, with people studying to become scientists, to become musicians, to become artists.

We have only scratched the surface of the human potential for creativity. So far, we only have outstanding geniuses something like once a century. You had Plato, Cusa, Kepler, Leibniz, Beethoven, Einstein, and a few others. And these were relatively rare phenomena. If we take the new road which is now on the horizon, then every child on this planet can have access to universal education, because there is enough to eat, and there is enough housing so that the child can study and is not distracted by poverty or by Pokemon Go, or some other idiotic thing. But the child can learn Classical music, *bel canto* singing, learn geography, learn astronomy, learn the history of the Universe, the history of mankind, universal culture. Love other cultures by knowing the beauty of Chinese painting, of Indian drama, of poetry from Persia.

Once you know these cultures, you cannot help but say this is actually enrichment. All racism would go, all xenophobia would go. The world community would just be working together for the common aims of mankind.

Developing breakthroughs like thermonuclear fusion power in the short term, space colonization in the short and medium term, and discovering new breakthroughs about which we now do not even have an inkling of how to ask the right question. We are not an Earth-bound system, by any means. The ecologists are always talking about finding solutions within Earth-bound systems. This is complete nonsense. Mankind is a species which naturally can develop the planet with infrastructure and open up landlocked areas on Earth, but the continuation of this infrastructure will be in near-Earth space. The Moon is the first target, and other objects such as asteroids will be studied. Eventually, we will have the means to take longer space flights to Mars and other bodies in space. We will become a human species where the beautiful idea of Vladimir Vernadsky that the noösphere will take over the biosphere more and more, will prevail. What he meant by that is that human discoveries, human scientific and technological innovation, will be what will rule and dominate the world more and more.

From that standpoint, the fact that China decided to put innovation in the center of their efforts, is really the right step in the right direction. I can see—and I hope to see this in my lifetime—that the relations among na-

The 'Ode to Joy' of Beethoven's 9th Symphony being performed at the G-20 Summit.

CCTV/youtube

tions will completely change, that you no longer look at everything which is foreign with an attitude of mistrust and xenophobia, but that people will become much more educated. They will be much more patriots and citizens of the world, world citizens, which will not be a contradiction, as was said by Friedrich Schiller 200 years ago. And that we will basically give up all those stupid habits which prevent our creative potential from unfolding. People will have intelligent discussions. They will have loving relations among themselves by furthering the interest of the other.

So, I think we are at the verge of becoming adult. I think right now that the human race is behaving like little uneducated, spoiled two-year-olds who kick the knee of your colleague, and scream and say, "This is my toy!" That's about the mental level of geopolitics.

I think that is not worthy of man. I think man is meant to be a creative species, fully loving each other. Therefore, the *Ode to Joy* that was played at the gala evening in Hangzhou is really the vision of the future.

Ross: Do you have any concluding remarks?
Zepp-LaRouche: Yes, I would like people to—I'm aware of the fact that what I'm talking about is not the mainstream opinion about China, and about all of these other countries. I would ask the audience, if you disagree with what I said, don't just dismiss it, but please take the effort to look into it yourself. Look at the speeches of Xi Jinping and the other leaders. Look at what China is doing. Study Confucius, and you will find out that there *is* indeed a completely different philosophy that is much, much closer to what the United States was when it was founded, than most people realize. Both in terms of economics, and also in the idea that the government should be there for the common good. This is an idea which almost has been lost in the last decades.

I think people should just not dismiss it. Once you are convinced that what I have said is true, help us to get the United States on-board. The United States needs a Silk Road. China has a plan to have 50,000 km of fast train lines by 2020. We have developed an extension of the Silk Road for the United States, with a huge system of fast trains connecting the East and the West Coasts, the North and the South. Build a couple of new cities in places in the United States which make sense. And there is no reason why the United States cannot be part of this. It's not anti-American. America should become part of it, and you should help to do this.

China Changes the Course of World History

by William Jones

"I have said and I still say: we send Missionaries to the Indies in order to preach revealed religion. This is good, but it seems we need the Chinese to send us Missionaries in turn, for us to learn the natural religion that we have almost lost."

—Gottfried Leibniz

Sept. 8—The G-20 (Group of Twenty) Summit on September 4th and 5th, which took place in Hangzhou, China, has changed the course of human history. For the very first time a comprehensive policy for global economic development was agreed to by all of the leading nations of the world. Simultaneously, agreements were reached on long-term planning, economic cooperation, scientific and technological innovation, and in-depth discussion took place on the issue of developing a new financial architecture to supersede the bankrupt trans-Atlantic financial system.

Also, for the first time in the history of the G-20, many poorer or "less developed" nations officially participated in the G-20 discussions, setting a precedent that all of the discussions were conducted, and all of the

wikipedia

The heads of state attending the Sept. 4-5 G-20 summit in Hangzhou, China. President Xi Jinping expanded the number of participants by inviting several developing sector heads of state.

agreements were decided, on behalf of all of mankind, not simply a limited group of nations.

The great credit for this accomplishment must be given to Chinese President Xi Jinping and to his advocacy, over the course of the past four years, of a "Win-Win" approach to resolving international conflicts and problems. The policies which were broadly accepted by the twenty most developed nations gathered at Hangzhou, and by the great majority of countries in the world, are policies which have been put forth, and fought for, by the Chinese leadership. Far from the realm of wishful thinking, these policies had been formulated largely by China, based on her own experience over the last four decades of rapid economic development. Since the 1970s, China has pulled over *700 million* of her own people out of poverty, a feat unequaled in the history of mankind.

Beginning with the "Reform and Opening Up" policy initiated by Chinese leader Deng Xiaoping in 1978, China has progressed to a point where it is now one of the most important economic powers in the world. This economic revolution, unprecedented in the history of the human race, has centered on the development of science and technology as the drivers of economic growth as rapidly as possible. Typifying the accomplishments of this effort was the 1990s construction of the first major trans-Eurasian rail line to be built since the trans-Siberian Railroad more than 100 years ago—the so-called Eurasian Land-bridge, which runs from Rotterdam, Holland to Lianyungang on the Chinese coast, close to the eastern end of the Great Wall—a route which totals more than 10,900 kilometers in length and passes through 30 countries.

A second Eurasian route was opened by Chinese President Xi Jinping in 2013, stretching from Chongqing, China to Duisburg, Germany, a distance of 11,179 kilometers. The Eurasian Land-bridge concept is, in fact, a policy created by Helga and Lyndon LaRouche. It had been adopted by China in 1996 at an international conference in Beijing at which Mrs. LaRouche presented a speech titled "Building the Silk Road Land-Bridge: The Basis for the Mutual Security Interests of

Xinhua

The number of China-to-Europe cargo trains has been rapidly increasing. After China adopted a new brand, China Railway Express, and systematized and uniformly organized its containers, China scheduled a June 8, 2016 departure of trains from eight Chinese cities (Chongqing, Chengdu, Zhengzhou, Wuhan, Changsha, Suzhou, Dongguan, and Yiwu) all on that same day, bound for European cities. President Xi Jinping and Polish President Andrzej Duda were on hand in Warsaw when one of the trains arrived in Warsaw on June 20. Previously, 1,700 trains had made the transcontinental voyage from China to Europe. There are presently more than 39 routes operating between all of China and all of Europe. Above, the China Railway Express which left the Chongqing station June 8.

Asia and Europe." What was accomplished at the Hangzhou G-20 Summit and the world directionality this now portends, is precisely coherent with the intent of the policy initiatives launched by the LaRouches in the 1990s, and which have been most recently addressed in the *EIR* Special Report *The New Silk Road Becomes the World Land-Bridge,* an in-depth report initiated by Helga Zepp-LaRouche and published in November, 2014. As Mrs. LaRouche points out in that Report, it is now time to extend Xi Jinping's "New Silk Road" initiatives to every corner of the globe, as the necessary basis for ending the perpetual warfare of the past decades with "peace through development." This is precisely the goal which was taken up at Hangzhou.

The Significance of Hangzhou

Why did China choose this particular city as the site of the first G-20 Summit it hosted? The first reason is its great beauty, situated as it is on the beautiful West Lake, an idyllic lake surrounded by mountains. Prior to his taking the office of President in China, Xi Jinping had been the provincial governor of Zhejiang Province, of which Hangzhou is the capital, for six years. The city's history dates back thousands of years.

Timothy Rush

Willows framing a West Lake bridge in Hangzhou.

As you view the beautiful West Lake, you can see many bridges. Each of the top ten scenic spots of the West Lake has its own unique charm, whether viewed up close or from a distance. Connecting them are the age-old and elegant bridges. The bridges are the very inspiration for the emblem of the summit. The G-20 is like a bridge that brings us together from different parts of the world. It is a bridge of friendship. From here we sail on the sea of friendship across the world, to enhance mutual trust and amity, and bring each other ever closer. It is a bridge of cooperation. Here we discuss plans, strengthen coordination, and deepen cooperation for win-win outcomes. It is also a bridge leading to the future. From here we will forge ahead like passengers in the same boat, and embrace an even brighter future.

The wonderful gala performance opening the Summit, choreographed by Zhang Yimou, China's best-known film director (who had also choreographed the opening of the Beijing Olympics), built on this theme presented by Xi, featuring Western and Chinese music, concluding with the final choral movement of Beethoven's Ninth Symphony to the words of Friedrich Schiller's "Ode to Joy," followed by a rendition of "Auld Lang Syne," composed to a text by the great Scottish poet Robert Burns, and sung by a Chinese children's chorus. This was accompanied by a brilliant water and light-show in the West Lake, with a display of Chinese fireworks lighting up the city.

The Background to the Summit

After the completion of the Rotterdam-Lianyungang rail link in 1992, China's vision for further Eurasian economic development was not fully followed through, due to the onset of the world financial crisis of 1997-98, a crisis sparked by western speculation against Asian currencies. But the idea never died, and within one year of his assumption of office as General Secretary of the Communist Party of China in November 2012, Xi Jinping announced his dual policy of a "New Silk Road Economic Belt" and a "21st Century Maritime Silk Road," which he calls the "Belt and Road Initiative."

The Belt and Road Initiative can be understood on a number of levels. The centerpiece of the initiative con-

President Xi told his guests at the banquet dinner for the G-20 leaders, that Hangzhou has hosted many foreign visitors through the centuries who were captivated by its beauty. He mentioned the Jesuit missionary Father Matteo Ricci, who visited Hangzhou during his long stay in China 400 years ago, where he eventually died in the midst of his missionary work. Xi noted that Ricci had come across the Chinese saying: "Above there is Paradise, and down below there is Suzhou and Hangzhou," and had written this in his diary.

"This is perhaps the first time a Westerner had made this Chinese saying known to a non-Chinese audience," Xi said. Xi also noted that the great Indian poet Rabindranath Tagore had also enjoyed his stay in Hangzhou and used it as the setting to some of his most beautiful poems.

Building Bridges

The choice of Hangzhou was also a political metaphor. President Xi told his G-20 dinner guests:

sists of major investment in the infrastructure of the neighboring countries in Central Asia and Southeast Asia, that is, roads, railroads, ports and the like. It is, on the one hand, a focussed "good neighbor policy" on the part of China.

Second, it allowed China to utilize what had become, with the collapse of the Western and other export markets, "excess industrial capacity" which could then be tapped to meet the needs of the neighboring countries, including even the transfer of physical industrial assets to the other countries for their own development.

Third, it would allow increased rapid transit of goods and people from the production centers in China to the European market, and vice versa. Xi's proposal quickly won broad support from many countries in the world.

aiib.org

Heads of delegations, representing the 57 prospective AIIB founding members, participating in the special ministerial meeting at the establishment of the AIIB in Beijing on June 29, 2015.

To facilitate these projects China took the lead in creating new financial institutions: the Asian Infrastructure Investment Bank (AIIB) and the BRICS Development Bank (now known as the New Development Bank). These institutions, unlike the U.S.-dominated World Bank and the U.S.- and Japanese-controlled Asian Development Bank, would be focussed solely on infrastructural (i.e., real physical economic) investment, without political *conditionalities.* For the first time since the 2008 financial crisis, the world was given a way out of the economic and banking morass.

The countries of the developing sector, focused especially around the alliance of the BRICS nations, suddenly saw a brighter future for themselves. Barack Obama and his London and Wall Street sponsors, who view themselves as the *Lords* of the global financial *Manor,* have tried to sabotage these new institutions by pressuring countries to remain outside them, but this effort has increasingly fallen on deaf ears. Even the British decided to join the AIIB, and now Canada, at the Hangzhou Summit, became the first North American country to join it. The United States is now the odd-man-out, along with Japan,— which is having second thoughts. Xi Jinping has insisted that the AIIB is not exclusive, and encouraged the United States and Japan to join.

While the new economic role that China has been playing for the last decade has been obvious to all except the most obtuse, the reality that emerged starkly from the G-20 Summit is the *political* leadership that China is now exerting. The program presented by the Chinese government for this year's G-20 has been signed on to by *all* the G-20 nations, including the United States. President Xi has named this the "Hangzhou Consensus."

Breaking a New Path to Growth

Innovation and development were the underlying themes of the Hangzhou gathering, the first time that these themes had been placed center-stage at a G-20 summit. This is part of China's broader effort to transform the G-20 from a crisis-response mechanism to a platform for long-term economic planning and coordination, to shift it from what President Xi characterized as a "talk shop" to an "action team." In his comments to business leaders at the Sept. 3 B-20 meeting, which preceded the G-20 Summit, Xi underlined the predominant issue: "As a Chinese saying goes, people with petty shrewdness attend to trivial matters, while those with greater wisdom attend to governance of institutions." Much of the content of the Hangzhou Summit was an attempt to raise the level of these world leaders from the level of geopolitical petty shrewdness closer to the level of wisdom.

Xi continued:

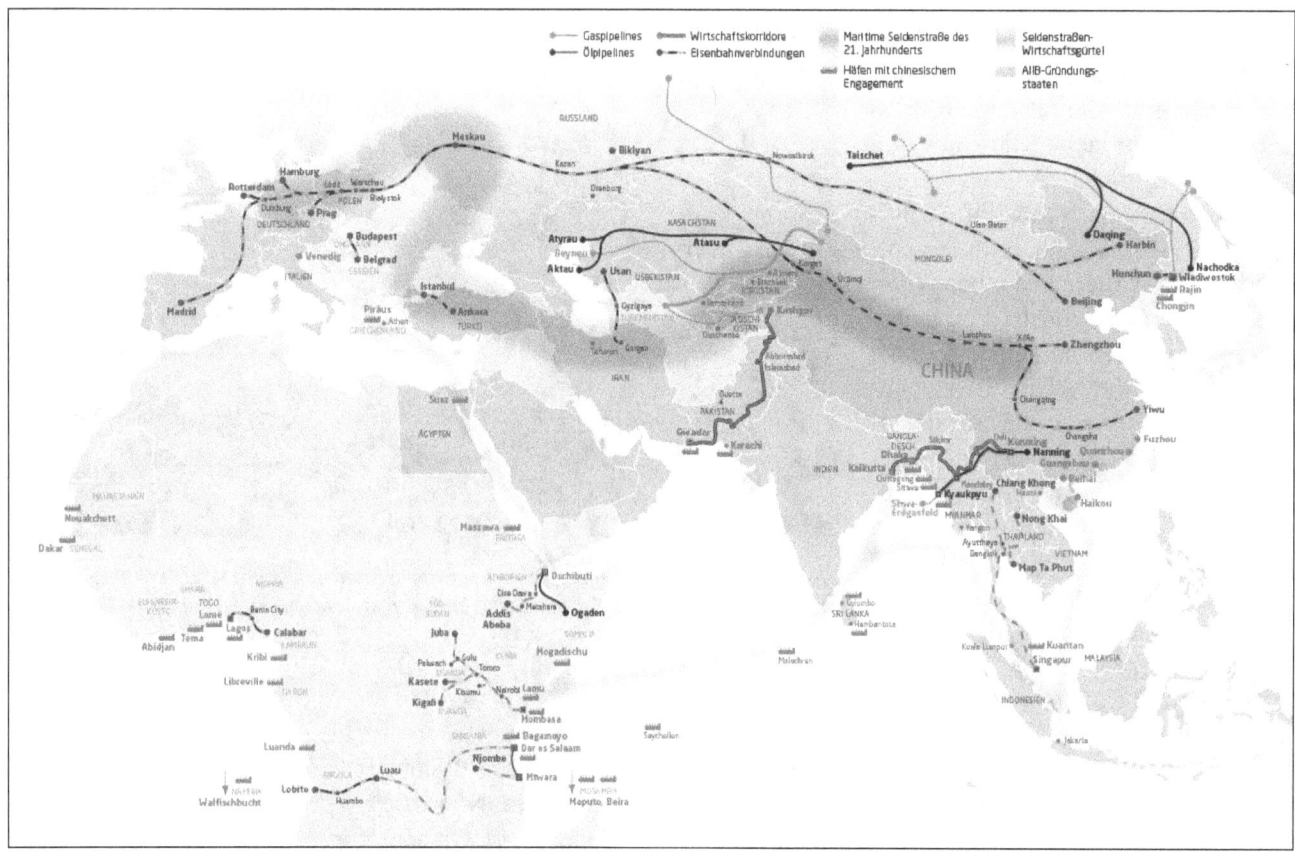

We need to seize the historic opportunity presented by innovation, the new scientific and technological revolution, industrial transformation, and the digital economy, to increase the medium and long-term growth potential of the world economy. This will be the first time that the G-20 takes action on innovation.... In light of the pronounced issue of lackluster global economic growth, we need to innovate our macroeconomic policies and effectively combine fiscal and monetary policies with structural reform policies.

Speaking at the concluding press conference on Sept. 5, Xi again returned to this theme, identifying the need for creative thinking in all areas of human practice.

Facing the current challenges, we can't rely on fiscal and monetary policies. We must envision an all-dimensional, multi-tiered and wide-ranging approach to innovation which is driven by innovation in science and technology, but goes beyond it to cover development philosophy, institutional mechanisms, and business models, so that innovation will be shared by all.

The Role of the Developing Countries

The second breakthrough that China introduced to the Hangzhou G-20 Summit was to invite non-G-20 countries to attend as observers—in particular from the developing-sector countries. There were heads of state or top leaders from Egypt, Thailand, Singapore, Senegal, Laos, Kazakstan and Saudi Arabia, as well as the G-20 leaders and leaders of international organizations representing the vast majority of the world's nations. This was in line with Xi's idea that the G-20 must not only represent their own countries, but must take responsibility for the entire world. Again at China's recommendation, the G-20 this year also placed, for the first time, the issue of the industrialization of Africa and the least developed countries (LDCs) as one of its priority items.

This was reflected in the importance that the Chinese organizers placed on the notion of interconnectedness and inclusiveness, two of the themes of the G-20, along with Innovation and Invigoration. Speaking to the B20 business leaders, President Xi said:

> In an age of economic globalization, countries are closely linked in their development, and they all rise and fall together. No country could seek development on its own, and the one sure path is through coordination and cooperation. We need to realize interconnected development, by promoting the common development of the world economy.

This was also expressed in the importance Xi placed on the meeting between the BRICS leaders (Brazil, Russia, India, China and South Africa), who held an informal meeting just prior to the G-20 plenary, in preparation for the upcoming BRICS Summit in India next month. "The rise of the developing countries is one of the most remarkable changes during the last decades," Xi told the BRICS.

The Group of 77, representing 134 less-developed nations, was represented by its current chairman, Thai Prime Minister Prayut Chan-Ocha, who called in his speech to the G-20 for cooperation between the two organizations, emphasizing that the proper agenda is precisely that put forth by Xi Jinping at the G-20—innovation, development, and inclusiveness.

wikimedia.org

Informal meeting of BRICS leaders on the sidelines of the 2016 G-20 Summit in Hangzhou, China.

Dealing with the Banking/Financial Crisis

A major focus for many of the G-20 members was the question of creating a new financial architecture that is truly beneficial to economic growth. President Xi said in his opening comments to the G-20:

> The world is facing multiple risks. There is the risk of excessive leverage and bubbles continuing to build up ... The G-20 should continue to improve the international monetary and financial systems and the governance structure of international financial institutions, and strengthen the global financial safety net to boost the resilience of the world economy against risks.

Most important, at the G-20 meeting there was a renewed emphasis placed on infrastructural investment. The model of the Belt and Road has pointed the way, but it is clear that China would like a broader emphasis on infrastructure from other international institutions, as they see this as the only road to development for the less-developed countries. Xi also noted that the G-20 Finance Ministers in their meeting in March, had concurred with the recommendation of China for a "Global Infrastructure Connectivity Alliance Initiative," an important step towards creating what Helga Zepp-LaRouche calls the World Landbridge.

Obama's Isolation

The momentum for a global shift toward a world development policy has been effected thanks to the effort of China and Russia and the BRICS countries. They have been adamant in changing the underlying assumptions governing economics, by putting at the center of economics the people's livelihood. As President Xi told the business leaders:

> The people are the foundation of a country, and only when the people lead a good life can the country thrive. We need to be people-oriented, a principle that we should follow in everything we do in advancing economic and social development.

An individual committed to a cynical world-view might question whether the governments of the twenty nations gathered at Hangzhou will continue to remain true to the commitments which they have made there, and it is certainly true that the enemies of progress will do their best to stop this momentum.

Nevertheless, one telling signal of what is to come, was the complete failure of President Barack Obama to block any of the Chinese proposals, or to effect any measures whatsoever to derail the momentum set into motion by China at the G-20. This attests to the solidity of the support that China has received for its initiatives. Even the Philippines, which had been playing along in Obama's geopolitical games against China, has now, under its newly elected President Rodrigo Duterte, refused to let the Philippines remain an obedient tool for their former colonial ruler. They see China's offer of infrastructure development and cooperation in the South China Sea, as preferable to Obama's austerity policies and a military buildup for war with China.

There was also a bilateral meeting between Xi Jinping and Japanese Prime Minister Shinzo Abe, the first in over a year. While China is most concerned about Abe's moves to remilitarize Japan's foreign policy, Xi told Abe that the two should work to bring relations onto a "normal track," while Abe said that Japan wants to work with China to promote global growth by "promoting win-win cooperation"—a term associated with Xi Jinping's global vision.

This is in keeping with the rapidly strengthening ties between Japan and Russia, centered on the new frontier represented by the Russian Far East. Abe recognizes that Japan's future critically depends on cooperation with Russia, as well as China, in the development of Asia as a whole in the world context. Just prior to the G-20 meeting, there was an important conference in Vladivostok which focused on the development of the Russian Far East, in which Abe played a central role, signing numerous deals with Russia in energy, transportation, and more.

With or Without America: the Momentum Will Not Stop

Speaking to reporters after the G-20, Russian President Vladimir Putin explained how the historic "Hangzhou Consensus" will work.

You know, of course, there are no decisions here that would be obligatory for the member countries. The G-20 does not take legally binding decisions. Many such formats do not take such decisions—in fact none of them do. However, the value of such discussions and such documents lies elsewhere. Their value is that they set a trend … If somebody moves in a different direction, he acts contrary to the wish of the global community and violates, as it were, generally accepted norms, even if they are not obligatory. These trends are very important. So there is a certain value in this and it is quite significant.

And the momentum will not stop. The day after the G-20 Summit, Chinese Premier Li Keqiang headed off to Laos for the ASEAN (Association of Southeast Asian Nations) Summit, as well as the ASEAN + 1 (ASEAN and China) and ASEAN + 3 (ASEAN-China-South Korea-Japan) meetings. 2016 is also the Twenty-Fifth anniversary of the ASEAN-China relationship, which was a subject of great celebration this year. The conclusions of the various summits in Laos were also fully in keeping with the new paradigm which emerged in Hangzhou—cooperation on infrastructure and development, with the Silk Road concept at the center.

As for the South China Sea, instead of allowing it to fester as a matter of contention, the final communique of the ASEAN Summit called for a negotiated settlement to all boundary disputes to be concluded between the nations in the region, without outside interference,— and other agreements were made at that summit for dealing with emergencies at sea, along with a commitment to conclude a code of conduct in the coming months.

The issue remains as to when the United States will come out of its "splendid isolation" and rejoin the rest of the world. The anger of the American electorate over the recent wars and financial crises ought to send a clear signal that they will no longer tolerate "business as usual."

So why not move in the direction opened up by China? China wouldn't need to send "Missionaries" to teach us the value of "innovation-led growth" if we were simply to return to the values we once held dear at the time we sent a man to the Moon, and if we indicate a willingness to work with China as an equal political partner—to begin to eliminate the poverty and misery that still hold the large bulk of mankind in their ugly grip.

II. Lyndon LaRouche at 94

Lyndon LaRouche Is the Soul Of the United States of America

The following comments were adapted from a presentation made on Sept. 8, 2016, the 94th birthday of Lyndon H. LaRouche, Jr., by William F. Wertz, Jr., on the La-Rouche PAC Fireside Chat.

September 8 is Lyndon LaRouche's 94th birthday. He was born in 1922. And he's probably the youngest one among us from the standpoint of his power of reason.

I think the basic point here is that the world is on the verge of seeing the fruition of what Lyndon LaRouche has fought for, steadfastly, over a period of decades: the development of a just, new world economic order, which is consonant with the actual nature of the human species as the only creative species. And we've seen these developments proceeding with great density and rapidity even over the last week: There was a conference in Vladivostok, the Eastern Economic Forum in Russia. It was followed by the G-20 Summit in Hangzhou, China, which was followed in turn by the ASEAN summit and the East Asia Summit in Vientiane, Laos. In addition, the UN General Assembly will begin on Sept. 13th. Later, on Oct. 15-16, the annual BRICS summit will take place in Goa, India.

What these developments represent is a commitment to an economic order which is oriented towards development of this planet and of the productive powers of all human beings, and at the same time a commitment to the exploration of space, which is mankind's true residence, in a certain sense, since we're not really earthlings, as Lyndon LaRouche has often said.

Coinciding with these events, there will be a Living Memorial for the victims of 9/11 this weekend in the greater New York area. This is the 15th anniversary of 9/11/2001 attacks. And the Schiller Institute New York Community Chorus will be performing Mozart's *Requiem* in four locations—starting on Friday in the Bronx, Saturday in Manhattan, Brooklyn on Sunday, and then Morristown, New Jersey on Monday night. These concerts are really designed again to bring justice to the fore, not only for the victims of 9/11 directly, but also, indirectly, for the victims internationally, which includes all of us, who are victims not only of the attacks, but also of the cover-up of the attacks and the further crimes facili-

LPAC

Lyndon H. LaRouche, Jr. participating in a recent LPAC TV Policy Committee broadcast.

tated by the attacks and the coverup. And this is something that Lyndon LaRouche had proposed that we have—a Living Memorial. And this is coming on only the second anniversary of Lyndon LaRouche having initiated what he called "the Manhattan Project."

We have these developments in the United States, which have a potential to change the United States of America at a crucial moment, and these developments in Manhattan are occurring at the same time that we have the development of the New Paradigm internationally, centered on Asia, but not limited to Asia. And all of this is occurring in the context of Lyndon LaRouche's birthday today, Sept. 8.

I want to urge people to think in terms of Lyndon LaRouche's actual significance, and this is not a significance which is merely in the past. This is his ongoing significance, it is a living significance because he is still active, in a way that redefines being active as being a creative force in the Universe. I think one can say that Lyndon LaRouche is the soul of the United States of America, and he has been so over these last several decades. This country would be in far, far worse shape if it had not been for the fight which Lyndon LaRouche has waged, going back to World War II, and perhaps even before that in high school, where he challenged false authority by refusing to accept the axiomatic assumptions of Euclidean geometry, because he knew that the universe was not based upon perfect linear extension but rather was characterized by curvature.

The New Ideas He Created

He wouldn't just accept things that most of us did accept as early as high school. He operated from the standpoint of the authority of the power of reason: You should only accept those things which you can actually prove through your own exercise of reason. It was Nicholas of Cusa who said that the soul is the power of reason, and that's why I said that Lyndon LaRouche *is* the soul of America, and that his importance to the world is highly underestimated. It's important for us to reflect on what he has done at the moment in which his work is coming to fruition. It's not that the results are finally in, it's not that the political war has been won once and for all, but the dynamic has now been established: The old system is passing away and the new system is coming into existence.

When the Soviet Union fell, there was a pseudo-intellectual by the name of Francis Fukuyama who wrote something called *The End of History and the Last Man,* and his whole thesis was that with the fall of the Soviet Union, British predatory capitalism had won, and therefore history had come to an end. And yet, everything that we see right now is just the opposite of that. This predatory British Empire capitalism is itself on the verge of suffering the same fate as that of the Soviet system previously.

Fukuyama's whole thesis was completely fraudulent. It reminds you of those who argue that the Creator created the Universe, and at that point there was nothing else the Creator either needed to do or could do. So what this Aristotelian view argued was that creativity was not an ongoing act of principle in the Universe. It was the philosopher Philo Judaeus of Alexandria who was the first to counter this view altogether.

What it brings out is the fact that man, as Lyndon LaRouche is insisting, is creative, and that creativity is not a linear extension of contributions from the past. A Renaissance is not merely a revival of that which had been known in the past. It is something completely new. As Lyndon LaRouche said about a week ago, "creativity is something which comes out of the blue." And that is what characterizes Lyndon LaRouche.

And we don't often advertise this now,— and I think that is a mistake,— but Lyndon LaRouche is foremost an economist. He is the most successful forecaster alive today, or actually who has ever existed. And in looking back, I mentioned his rejection of Euclidean geometry, but one of the things that comes to mind when you look at Lyndon LaRouche's history, is his rejection of the writings of Norbert Wiener, particularly of a book called *The Human Use of Human Beings: The Cybernetics of Society.* And what Wiener—I don't think he's related to the other notorious Wiener from New York today—argued is that the Universe is entropic. And again, this is something which most people in society accept, all the institutions accept it: They believe that the Second Law of Thermodynamics is universally valid, and that entropy increases. And all of the false ideology which has become predominant in the world, especially since the 1960s but even before that, is based on this false notion of the primacy of entropy.

Lyndon LaRouche,— and this is a crucial turning point as he relates it in his autobiography, *The Power of Reason,*— upon his reading of Wiener, rejected this notion as emphatically as he had rejected the related notions of Euclid. What Wiener argues in that book is that the Universe is entropic and even if you have a negative-entropic, or a negentropic development locally,

EIRNS/Stuart Lewis

Schiller Institute chorus performing Mozart's Requiem at the Co-Cathedral of St. Joseph, Brooklyn, NY, as part of a four-concert living memorial by the Schiller Institute, on the weekend of 9/11/2016, to victims of the 9/11/2001 attacks.

you can counter entropy locally for a short period of time, but the more successfully you counter entropy, the more rapidly entropy will exert itself and exert itself more viciously. For Wiener, progress itself is counter-productive, in that it leads to increased entropy.

So this is a complete denial of humanity's creativity and the fact that through human creativity, man is a force in the Universe which is anti-entropic, and that the nature of the Universe itself is anti-entropic as opposed to entropic. This, I think is really the crucial distinction that Lyndon LaRouche arrived at, which led him then to his economic forecasts, starting in the 1950s, and his development of the LaRouche-Riemann method of Economics, in which he laid out the perspective that man's development in the Universe is characterized by his making scientific discoveries, creative discoveries, and those being implemented in terms of technology so as to develop capital-intensive modes of production which redefine the resource base and allow for an increase in what Lyndon LaRouche called the

potential relative population-density.

He Never Stopped Fighting

The latter is a scientific term which he invented. It didn't exist before. It expresses the fundamental anti-entropic principle of human nature and of human economy, which runs completely counter to the idea that we're now in a post-industrial society: We don't have to develop industry; we don't have to go to the Moon, as Barack Obama said, because "we've been there, done that." LaRouche's idea rejects the whole notion that there are limits to growth. It's a rejection of the idea that we're suffering from overpopulation, because what we're actually suffering from is underpopulation and the failure to develop the mental powers of the population.

These conceptions are fundamental to Lyndon La-Rouche's breakthrough in economic science, which, as he put it, is the queen of all the sciences, because it's the basis for human existence. And in that sense, I would maintain that Lyndon LaRouche's contribution in terms of economics is the underpinning of the New Paradigm which is now in the process of establishing itself on this globe, and is the only hope which we in the United States have, to the extent to which we move to get Glass-Steagall passed, to implement LaRouche's Four Cardinal laws, and to bring the United States into this Asian geometry.

Everything positive that's occurring right now in the world is something that Lyndon LaRouche and Helga LaRouche have fought for. For instance, if you look at his *Power of Reason* book which was published in 1988, the final chapters are on "Asia, the New Economic Frontier," on the space program, and also on his marriage to Helga Zepp-LaRouche, and the importance of that in terms of what they have commited their marriage to, over these succeeding years.

Now the only way that we're going to take back this country, given what's passing for a Presidential election, is the extent to which we create a movement in this country. And that means not just mobilizing yourself, but mobilizing other people to fight for the country. That's why I started out with the question of Lyndon LaRouche's importance to this country. You have look at his history. After World War II, many people came back and they just gave up the fight. They had fought fascism, whether it was Japanese militarism or the Nazis, and they came back and they found the country had been taken over through Truman, resulting in the period of McCarthyism. They then ran from the fight which they had just devoted themselves to internationally.

Lyndon LaRouche did not give up that fight. He knew the importance of what Roosevelt did, and he knew that Truman would take the country in the opposite direction. He met with other soldiers who approached him in India, where they were after Roosevelt had died, and he told them he was very concerned because a "great man has been replaced by a small man."

So here you have an individual, all by himself, coming back to the United States, not giving up that fight, developing himself as an economist during the 1950s, developing his first economic forecast of a recession in the late 1950s and continuing along these

EIRNS/Alan Yue

1971 debate of Lyndon LaRouche (with pipe) with Abba Lerner (standing).

lines. Then he gets into the 1960s and he recognizes that there are no real institutions which are fighting for this country and for humanity. In the late 1960s, he intervened against the New Left and created what was called at that point, the National Caucus of Labor Committees, an independent organization, the core of which still exists to this day!

In other words, he was combatting people who were saying, at that point, that there couldn't be another Depression, "because we have built-in stabilizers." But LaRouche said, no, this economic policy is leading not only to recession but an economic collapse. This was demonstrated by what happened on Aug. 15, 1971: Nixon announced that he was going to abandon the Bretton Woods fixed-exchange-rate system set up by Franklin Roosevelt, that he was going to decouple the dollar from the gold reserve system, and that he was going to impose price and wage controls and austerity.

At that point, LaRouche argued in a major article in our newspaper of that time, that either we go forward with what he called at that point "expanded social reproduction," which was his conception of economic development, or we're facing fascism. And in that year, he had a debate with a liberal economist by the name of Abba Lerner at Queens College. And in the debate Lyn, not through debaters' points, but rather by just developing the truth, forced Abba Lerner to come out and say that if Germany had followed the policies of Hjalmar Schacht, "then Hitler wouldn't have been necessary."

But who was Hjalmar Schacht? Hjalmar Schacht

Presidential candidate Lyndon LaRouche (left) conversing with Presidential candidate Ronald Reagan at a campaign event in New Hampshire in 1980.

was the guy who helped bring Hitler into power, and then as Economics Minister under Hitler implemented the fascist austerity policies Hitler needed to enforce.

So the point was that LaRouche confirmed his analysis by defeating Abba Lerner in this debate, and LaRouche's organization grew by leaps and bounds during this period. The basic thrust was *against* the ideology of the New Left, because the New Left believed in limits to growth, they believed there was overpopulation, they believed that we're in a post-industrial society. That was their ideology, an ideology which is in fact fascist.

And you go forward from there, and Lyn continued to fight, not only in the United States but internationally, and this is one man doing this, fighting for a policy of economic development, putting forward his proposal for an International Development Bank. In 1976, the Non-Aligned Movement had its summit in Colombo, Sri Lanka, at which the Foreign Minister of Guyana Fred Wills, with whom we had been in contact, gave a speech calling for a moratorium on Third World debt so that you could actually have economic development of the Third World. This was a result of the influence of LaRouche.

And LaRouche then decided to run for President against Jimmy Carter. He did a half-hour TV show, exposing the policies of Jimmy Carter as destructive to this country and endangering the world by bringing it to the brink of thermonuclear war. By the late 1970s, some of the people in the intelligence community who had worked with Roosevelt, began to work with LaRuche, and he became the person, even before Ronald Reagan

was inaugurated, who was formulating policy for the new Administration, including what later became the Strategic Defense Initiative (SDI) enunciated by Reagan.

And the enemy couldn't stand that, and so you had the assassination attempt against Reagan, and then after the '84 election, in which LaRouche ran again, you had persecution of Lyndon LaRouche and his associates, and the jailing of LaRouche in 1989 by the Bush forces.

And yet, he comes out of jail, and he continues to fight! How many people would do that? What is the quality of his mind that led him to continue to fight like that? When the people who served with him in World War II gave up the fight, he continued to fight. He then formed the LaRouche organization all by himself in the 1960s and '70s. He was then thrown into jail and came out of jail and continued to fight. And he is still continuing this fight at the age of 94. I think you have to look at the fact that he is motivated by an actual commitment to creativity—his own creativity and the evocation of the creativity of others, on behalf of humanity and humanity's mission.

And it's that quality which we have to find in ourselves and evoke in other people, that sense of mission, being willing to combat public opinion, to think through and make sure you're right, but to stand even if you have to stand alone on behalf of what is true—that's the quality that Lyndon LaRouche represents. There are very few people throughout history who have that quality and who are actually creative in the real sense of being creative.

I was thinking of what he had said the other day, in a private conversation, about how creativity is not based upon reviving great ideas from the past and building on them, but rather it's developing something completely new. And one example that comes to my mind is Nicholas of Cusa, who proved that you could not square a circle, as Archimedes had said you could. Archimedes' assumption was that you could square the circle, that you could come up with an approximation through inscribing a polygon within a circle.

Nicholas of Cusa's discovery wasn't the linear extension of Archimedes. It was a rejection of Archimedes, and a discovery of the fact that circular action is ontologically superior to polygonal action, because it's not linear. For instance, if you have a circle you can create a square by folding the circle twice. And you can create other polygonal figures within a circle. But you cannot go from a polygon to creating a curved circumference. So the circle is actually transcendental in relationship to a polygon. And that was a completely new discovery! It had never existed in human history before.

And that's the quality of thinking that's actually required: You find that in Einstein, you find that in some other individuals. And that quality is really what we have to make clear to people, this is what really makes people human, and this is what we need to advance humanity, this kind of thinking.

And so, in organizing others to organize, we have to also really look in this deeper level as well. There's an immediate necessity for action on Glass-Steagall just as there was to declassify the 28 pages on 9/11. But at the same time, there's a deeper understanding that we have to have of what mankind requires, and develop that in ourselves and encourage that in others. Throughout much of his life, Lyndon LaRouche has been demonized. He was railroaded and thrown into prison, and you have to appreciate what he's done and what he represents for the future. This country is in bad shape, but think about what shape it would be in if it were not for the fact that Lyndon LaRouche has played this central role in the history of this country over the last several decades. The possibility of shifting the direction of the United States would not exist, if it were not for Lyndon LaRouche.

And then I think in that context, it's important to really reflect upon what it is about him that has allowed him to do that. Because I think we all owe him a debt of gratitude. But it's not just a question of saying "thanks." It's a question of really thinking about what he continues to do, and thinking through what it's necessary for each of us to do, in terms of our own contribution, but also in terms of helping to develop a society where others can emerge who have the quality which he has had, and which is essential for humanity.

It's not just the immediate actions that are necessary,—as necessary as those are. It's also necessary to reflect upon this deeper question. And I know that that's what people are going to be thinking about this weekend, in the New York area, with the performance of Mozart's *Requiem*, which is a profound reflection of man's immortality. And it's that immortality which you have to have in your mind's eye as you go through life, as Lyndon LaRouche continues to do.

III. The Truth About Syria

VIRGINIA STATE SENATOR RICHARD BLACK

'We Are Better Than This, Let's Change Our Government's Direction'

Virginia State Senator Richard Black spoke at the New York Sept. 10 Schiller Institute Conference: "Securing World Peace through Enhancing the Common Aims of Mankind." This is an edited transcript.

Moderator Dennis Speed: I think everyone in this audience is aware that there has been an extensive battle around the question of Syria.

The next speaker has distinguished himself by being one of the few Americans who has taken on the corruption of the policy of the United States, and expressed his view of that policy directly and forthrightly. He is a State Senator from Virginia. It is my honor to introduce to you State Senator Richard Black.

Richard Black: Thank you very much. Thank you. I appreciate it very much. I'm going to talk to you about the background of the Syrian war, particularly on the issues of the moderate rebels and American involvement in this.

First of all, I want to let you know a little about me. I am a conservative Republican and I have very extensive combat experience. I have been wounded in action, had my radio man killed right beside me in battle, flew

EIRNS/Stuart Lewis
Virginia State Senator Richard Black addressing the Sept. 10 Schiller Institute Conference in New York City.

269 combat missions, and then, later, I served in the Pentagon on the general staff. I was a JAG officer advising the Senate Armed Service Committee, working on executive orders for the President, and testifying before committees in Congress. I come at this from a little different perspective than some people do. I just wanted to give that as background.

First of all, let me go back in time, and I'd like you to know a little bit about Syria and what Syria was like before the war began. Before the war, Syria was the safest of all Arab countries. There weren't any kidnappings, you could walk freely anywhere. It was a tremendously friendly place. There had been 40 years of peace with Israel, and interestingly, they had the greatest women's rights of any Arab country. There was total religious freedom in Syria.

I think Syria is unique in the entire world, in terms of religious harmony. Not tolerance, where you are putting up with something you dislike, but a certain love among people of the Muslim faith, the Christians, the Alawites, really truly an amazing atmosphere. I visited with President Bashar al-Assad for a couple of hours during a trip I took to Syria this year. He is an interesting individual: he is a very thoughtful, very brilliant man, soft spoken, almost a touch shy in a sense.

His wife, Asma al-Assad, is just a joyous woman, extremely bright. She was an investment banker, raised in London. And when the two of them took over in Syria, they came in with this zeal. They are young people, idealistic people, and they had a zeal for transforming Syria, rooting out corruption, improving the economy and so forth. Little did they know there were things under way that were going to prevent that.

I want to get one thing out of the way right up front. All of you have heard, probably a thousand times, that President Assad gassed his own people, that he used sarin gas in Damascus, that he crossed the red line. Well, this is totally incorrect, and this particular 2013 time-line will show you that all of this occurs in a three-month period. You go to March 30. In Turkey there was a series of raids. Thirteen al-Qaeda homes were raided by Turkish border authorities within Turkey. They did the raids based on probable cause that resulted from extensive wiretaps in which they recorded the fact that the al-Qaeda operatives were moving major supplies of sarin gas into Syria from Turkey. The precursor chemicals came from Western Europe,— I'm not sure which country, but it came out of the West,— so Western Europe, NATO was complicit in this. Anyway, these people were all arrested.

And then President Erdogan ensured that there was a new prosecutor assigned, the case was dismissed, and individuals crossed the border into Syria.

Okay, that was on May 30. On June 20, the Defense Intelligence Agency, which is probably one of the most respectable agencies of the United States government,— it comes under the Chairman of the Joint Chiefs of Staff,— they issued a report saying that Al-Nusra has major sarin production units in operation. This is coming out of the Pentagon at a very high level.

Syria Was a Stable Country

You go to Aug. 13. This is a very, very odd day. The rebels, the terrorists, whatever you want to call them, called together a very important meeting that included the CIA, MI6, various representatives from Saudi Arabia, Qatar, and all of those who have been so deeply involved in this war. They announced that there would be a war-changing development,— *and* that the United States would bomb Syria.

Now think about this. *Rebels* announced—here is the Ghouta gas attack [of Aug. 21]. Rebels announced eight days before the Ghouta gas attack that there would be an important event that would cause the United States to bomb Damascus and enter the war openly. I have difficulty believing there were not representatives of the United States government who were in the know, because we held enormous supplies of weapons in warehouses in Turkey, the keys held by CIA. Based on that meeting, we *immediately* began transferring *immense* quantities of our most advanced weapons to the terrorists across the border in Syria.

Now look: Aug. 21, the Ghouta gas attack which all of you heard about. Of all things, Syria, which was engaged in probably five multiple battle fronts where there was a desperate struggle going on, somehow chose to cross the red line by firing sarin gas at civilian targets. That's irrational. I'm going to tell you President Assad is not an irrational person. If he had been willing to have the United States enter the war, if he was willing to risk that, he *certainly* would not have wasted the chemicals. He certainly would have used it on the battle front where he could have at least turned the tide of battle.

The weapons all arrived somewhere between Aug. 21 and 23. As you can imagine, it takes a tremendous logistic effort to get these things there. So that leaves us the question: How did the rebels know the United States was going to bomb Syria? A very disturbing question, I think.

The answer to this—Turkey and Al-Qaeda executed the gas attack. We have significant evidence of this. First, we know that the 2.2 kilograms were seized. This was widely reported. This occurred three months before the red line gas attack. Also, if you really want to become educated, read the writings of Pulitzer Prize winning author Seymour Hersh. He is the guy that broke the story on the My Lai massacre during the Vietnam War, and he analyzes in great depth how Turkey and Al-Qaeda executed the sarin gas attack, blaming it on Bashar al-Assad for the purpose of pulling the United States openly into the war.

Now, this is sort of the icing on the cake. The other things you can say, these are coincidental or circumstantial. However, in December 2015, Turkish members of Parliament,— two individuals, incredibly heroic, at great risk to their lives,— held an extensive press conference in which they laid out all of the evidence that had been seized by Turkish authorities—the wiretap information—and they disclosed how Turkey

EIRNS/Stuart Lewis

Senator Black describing how Al-Qaeda carried out the gas attack against civilians in Syria with Turkish involvement.

had sent the sarin gas, and the rockets, to deliver them into Syria for the purposes of provoking the U.S. attack. Those people were immediately charged with treason for revealing state secrets. And I'm going to tell you what: in Turkey, if you cross the government, in such a significant way, your life is not worth a plugged nickel. So I've got to hand it to these people. Anybody who thinks that that is not proof beyond reasonable doubt, I'm going to tell you, those guys are likely to die for what they did. God bless them. They are true heroes.

Now, we have all heard that the Syrian war began with the Arab Spring in 2011. That's when it occurred, in 2011. The fact is, the Syrian war countdown begins immediately after 9/11. Gen. Wesley Clark, the former Supreme Allied Commander Europe, has stated very unequivocally on videos that he was in the Pentagon and he was informed that there was a top-secret document that had come down, and that the Pentagon had been instructed to draft plans to overthrow seven Arab governments within the next five years. This is not some remote source. This is the Supreme Allied Commander of Europe saying that. This is the senior four-star general outside of the Pentagon.

Five years pass. WikiLeaks—God bless them. I'll tell you what. At first I was a little reluctant, but now the more I read the documents and see the onion peeled away, the happier I am to see the information. In 2006, the U.S. Embassy drafted detailed plans on how to destabilize and overthrow Syria. Now, remember, there were no demonstrations. This was a stable country. It really was sort of the ideal in the Arab world, of what we would hope they would have, in terms of freedom, and women's rights, and things of that sort. But we had decided they were going to go down, and the plans were drafted.

We Opened Pandora's Box

One of the most sinister and unpleasant things about it, was that part of the plan involved creating religious divisions and hatred, where they did not exist. Because, as you have heard before and you will hear again, Syria had this atmosphere of religious harmony, unique in all of the world—honestly.

Okay, 2011: By then, Hillary Clinton is the Secretary of State. Now most people think that the Department of Defense starts wars. The DOD does not start wars. They are the executive agency. They carry out the orders given. It is the State Department/CIA,— which are really one and the same,— they are the ones who concoct the wars, draft the propaganda, and so forth. So, 2011, this is when I got involved, because we launched an unprovoked attack on Libya. We had had our problems with them, but we resolved them some six or eight years earlier. Colonel Qaddafi was our number-one ally in the war on terror in North Africa. Libya was the most prosperous of all North African countries, on a per-capita basis.

We launched an attack that utterly destroyed Libya. Libya does not have a government. There are various groups we recognize from time to time. Last year, the Libyan government had to meet in a ship offshore, because they could not control a ten-acre plot of the country of Libya. That is not a government. So there is no government; the place has been utterly crushed and destroyed. Why did we do it? I thought it was perhaps oil, and began to look into it. I came to discover the reason was that Qaddafi had a very large store of advanced weapons. We needed them to overturn Syria.

A month later, after the Libyan uprising, the Syrian uprising and the Syrian war begins. One month apart. Let's look at the causes of the war in Syria. Okay, some people have said, "oh it's a domestic uprising." I'll tell you, I have spoken to people who were demonstrators and they said, "initially"—you know, all of us have probably been involved in a demonstration of some sort. Pro this or anti that, or whatever. That's the kind of demonstrations that took place. They weren't trying to bring down the government.

But what happened is very shortly al-Qaeda flags began to show up at the demonstrations. They said, we don't want al-Qaeda flags. Then, automatic military weapons showed up, and they said "get rid of those, we don't want that." They don't have a Second Amendment in Syria. You don't go down to the corner drug store and buy a Kalashnikov. It doesn't happen. They come from somewhere. They come from covert intelligence agencies.

The third thing that happened is that they began to proselytize religious hatred. They began to exploit these little fractions, and there are always religious differences among people. I spoke with one fellow, and he said, "my uncle was the head of the demonstrators." "He kept trying to push these elements out. In the seventh month Al-Qaeda murdered him." So it was not a domestic uprising.

However, Saudi Arabia for many years had wanted to run an oil pipeline across Syria, and they had been unsuccessful in getting Syria's agreement to allow them to do this. Then, as the war approaches, Qatar, which,—their only product is natural gas,— it is a country that is basically sand dunes and gas wells. There is nothing else there. My wife Barbara and I have been there and seen it. So they asked for a gas pipeline. Syria refused the gas pipeline, and this immediately caused a flood of wealth starting to move from Qatar to the rebels in Syria.

The other thing I would say was an element of this was the weaponization of religion. This is something that the United States, unfortunately, began triggering during the conflict in Afghanistan with the Soviet Union. We began to create this mujahideen movement,

and we armed it, and when we found out that it was not big enough to overthrow the Soviet Union, we then worked with Saudi Arabia, CIA, and to some extent Pakistani Intelligence, and they set up these madrassas, and they taught, not the mainstream Islam, but Wahhabism. It was extremely violent, and we had, at that point, opened Pandora's box.

There Are No Moderate Rebels

And we have continued—you would think we would have learned our lesson and said, "Hey this is really dangerous. Put the top on the box." But instead we said, "Gosh, this is kind of neat. We can create hatreds between this group and that group and fissures, and we can use it in Iraq and we can use it everywhere." It is one of the most terrible things that has ever been done. And ironically it wasn't done by Osama bin Laden, it wasn't done by some terrorist, it was done by planners at the Central Intelligence Agency, who looked at the possibilities that were available, *if we could create these religions divisions*. And now, of course, they have gotten well out of hand.

Here are the competing oil and gas pipelines. Those are the ones favored by Saudi Arabia and Qatar. Iran had a plan to do one, also. Neither of those have been built as a result of the war.

If you read the works of Seymour Hersh, he wrote "The Red Line and The Rat Line," a magnificent article and if you are interested in this, you have got to look it up: "The Red Line and the Rat Line." The Red Line was Obama's threat to enter the war if poison gas was used. Very convenient. And it tied right in with what the Turks were doing. The other thing was the Rat Line. The Rat Line was the movement of Libyan weapons into Syria. This is the way it went. Qatar had a major air fleet. They sent transports into Libya. They were loaded with weapons. The weapons were transported to Turkey, and Turkey then funneled them across the border into Syria, where they supplied all sorts of terrorist groups.

Now, this became a major concern for the Pentagon. And the chairman of the Joint Chiefs of Staff directed the Defense Intelligence Agency to do a very extensive, highly classified project, to determine where we stood in Syria. The concern was that if Syria fell, the Pentagon believed it had major strategic implications for the entire Middle East, and perhaps beyond. The DIA rendered findings in the middle of 2013. Here is what they found: They said, first of all President Assad must remain in power or Syria will collapse in chaos, just as Libya has done. Next, they said that if Assad falls, he will be replaced by extremists.

Now, the CIA had ostensibly formed this rat line to supply moderate rebels. The Defense Intelligence Agency determined that by 2013 the Central Intelligence Agency was giving full support to all rebels, including Al-Qaeda and ISIS: the entire spectrum. Importantly, DIA determined that *there are no moderate rebels*. They do not exist. That is not to say there is not some fellow out there on the battlefield, but for any practical purposes, the moderate rebels do not exist. As a consequence, the United States is arming extremists.

Courtesy of Sen. Black

Senator Black at the ruins of Palmyra, a World Heritage Site that has been liberated from ISIS.

Now, this is the Defense Intelligence Agency, this is not my speculation or some particular group. The DIA warned of dire consequences from toppling Assad, and they repeatedly warned the White House of the dramatic strategic danger we faced if this were done. Lt. Gen. Michael Flynn was the commander of DIA. He was their director during the relevant time, and here is a quote from him:

> The Administration's policy was contradictory. They wanted Assad to go, but the opposition was dominated by extremists. We knew this, the White House knew it, and we forged on.

Here is where we are today. We've got a question, who will win the war in Syria? Well, first of all, we know it is not going to be the moderate rebels. We have a Defense Intelligence Agency finding that the moderate rebels do not exist. So it is not going to be them! Have I made that point? [Laughter.] All right.

There are two alternatives. President Assad, who is heavily supported by the army, who is heavily supported by the people of Syria, either they will win, or Al-Qaeda and associated groups—there is a whole panoply of groups, they all take different names—I can't help but believe that the use of these names is designed to make things so complex that ordinary people can't comprehend it, and they give up and say, OK, whatever

the government says. But the fact is, that the moderate rebels are no different from Al-Qaeda.

How Palmyra Fell to ISIS

Those are our two choices: Al-Qaeda or the government that is in power in Syria today. So you have to ask the question: Are we prepared for Al-Qaeda to take over Syria? We have experience with Al-Qaeda. We are about to celebrate the 15th anniversary of Al-Qaeda bringing down the Twin Towers and turning the Pentagon into a fireball. What awaits the Christians, the Alawites, the moderate Sunnis, the Shi'ites, the Druze? We know what will happen if Al-Qaeda takes over, because we have *seen* what happens when Al-Qaeda takes over, and this is the fate that awaits the good people, the decent people of Syria, what you see right here.

I have to go back to this idea: Syria has this magnificent tradition of religious harmony. This is in 2013. The war had been going on for two years. They erected a magnificent statue of Jesus Christ that overlooks Israel, Lebanon, and Syria. Can you imagine the difficulty we would have in this country, if we did it? [laughter] You can't do that in America! You have to do it in Syria! I had to go to Syria to experience the religious freedom that I knew when I was a child!

I spoke with the Grand Mufti. He's the leader of all of the Sunnis and I think to a good extent to the Shi'ites as well. Magnificent, wonderful man! He made the comment,—now there are 23 million Syrians — he said, "We Syrians are 23 million Christians." He said, "My mother's name was Myriam, like Mary, mother of Jesus."

Then I went and spoke with the Patriarch, the Christian Patriarch of Syria and the East, and he made the comment, he said, "We Syrians are 23 million Muslims." And when he said that I said, "That's interesting you say that, it's the reflection of what the Mufti said." And he stroked his beard, and he said, "Well, some people say I have a Muslim beard."

This is a reflection of the *love* and the affection,—it is genuine—between people of different faiths.

I went to a choral presentation one evening, and I was *stunned*. This is in a 70% Muslim city, the city of Homs, and all of a sudden, I'm watching and I couldn't tell what they were singing about,— they were singing in Arabic,— but they were singing about Christ's crucifixion, death, resurrection, ascension. It was the Christian Easter, and here they were, and I leaned over to the wife of the governor of Homs province, who is a Muslim, and said, "this is kind of surprising to me." She said, "Oh, many of the members of the choir and many of the members of the audience are Muslim as well."

Where else? Where else, but in Syria? This is on the final day of my visit. I gave an extensive interview to SANA, which is like the Fox News of Syria, and as I was walking out, I looked over, and here's a Christmas tree in the press pit, and I said "What is this?" And they said "This is the martyrs' Christmas tree."

You'll see the photographs there. There are seven people. All of them have been killed reporting on the Syrian war, which has been *horrific*. I mean this was like the American Civil War with the percentage of people slaughtered. And it occurred to me, I said here's a Christmas tree, there is a star on the top of it, it's even got the Christmas Grinch on there somewhere. And most of the pictures there are Muslims. It's sort of like, the Christians' way of honoring the Muslims for what they have done. So, it is unique in Syria.

Now, I went out to Palmyra. Palmyra is very interesting. It is one of the architectural gems of the entire world. And ISIS had captured it and the generals were showing me how they had managed to recapture, it once the Russians came in with an expeditionary force

courtesy of Sen. Richard Black

A Christmas-tree-shaped cutout in Homs as a memorial to journalists, most of whom are Muslim, who have been killed in Syria.

that provided some additional air support. Tremendously heroic people. And they had captured it.

However, ISIS had been allowed to capture Palmyra, and you can see the devastation. This was truly one of the architectural wonders of the world. It wasn't just a possession of Syria. It was a possession of all mankind, and it was allowed to be destroyed by ISIS. It just angered me, and I think you can see that when I'm talking to the press. Because we had a coalition of 67 nations, with aircraft that were supposedly working against ISIS, and ISIS was able to assemble a huge army—now let me just back up a second.

The Meaning of Aleppo

ISIS had to travel 100 miles across open desert, with hundreds and hundreds of vehicles—tanks, artillery pieces, trucks, all of these things. I cannot imagine that that coalition did not have the ability to spot everything that was going on, and I have confirmed they did not drop *one single bomb* to stop ISIS from taking Palmyra. Why? Because Palmyra is mid-way between the areas controlled by ISIS, and Damascus itself.

And I believe that we were so intent on toppling the government of Syria that we were willing to have ISIS, after all of the viciousness and horrors they had inflicted, we were willing to inflict that on Damascus, Syria, and to empower them with a far greater Caliphate than they had ever had. And it just infuriated me, and I think you can tell from the look on my face, my emotions there.

Now this will just give you some idea of where the war stands. If you look, the Syrian government—the government-controlled areas are shown in the reddish-orange there—they control 75-80% of the population of Syria. Much of Syria is desert. The white area is simply desert. It had very little population. The gray area is the area that was controlled by ISIS. It's gradually shrinking. You can see where Palmyra is, right in the center, right here. So you can see—they had to travel with a huge army across the desert to Palmyra, and we *deliberately* allowed them to do it, so that they could capture Palmyra, hoping that they would drive on to Damascus.

Now, just to bring you very current, the biggest battle that is taking place in Syria today is the battle for Aleppo. Aleppo is the industrial heartland of Syria. The rebels have held about 20% of the city for years. The government has held the vast majority of the city, but Al-Qaeda controls it—it's called Al-Nusra over there, but it's Al-Qaeda. Even the White House has said they're Al-Qaeda. And they had a supply route that went into the pocket and supplied it. And the Syrian army had tried for many years to try to seal that off. They finally attacked and they were able to do that, and they cut the supply line, and they created the Aleppo pocket.

Now, if you listen to the American mainstream media, you would think that all that's happening with Aleppo is that some civilians are in there, and they're just being bombed for no purpose whatsoever. The fact of the matter is, we really should be rejoicing, because there is a major al-Qaeda army that is trapped in there, and particularly on 9/11, we should say—Rah, here we go! We've trapped Al-Qaeda! We're going to get even with these people that brought down the Twin Towers, and sent people leaping from the flaming buildings, and leaping to their death a quarter of a mile below.

But anyway, the next thing is that Al-Qaeda assembled an army of 40,000 people. Now you won't know this from the mainstream media! 40,000 troops! That's *two* heavy American divisions,—and Al-Qaeda, they've done really well. They started with 19 people on 9/11; now they're up to two, full armored, mechanized divisions, and what they did is, they attacked. The forces inside attacked, and the forces outside attacked. Now, let me tell you. If you think for a moment that the Aleppo pocket is simply civilians, they attacked with *thousands* of terrorists, supported by 95 main battle tanks. 95 tanks!

This is one of the biggest armored battles in our lifetimes—not a word of it in the media. You've got to really dig and find it out. That's a lot of tanks.

But anyway, they managed to briefly breach the barrier, but the Syrian Army very, very skillfully drove them back, and have driven both of those arrows back, and they now have resealed the Aleppo pocket. And because they can't obtain new weapons and supplies inside, they're withering very quickly. The Syrian army is moving very quickly, and it appears that, absent something extraordinary, they have lost the battle of Aleppo.

I just want to let you know who these people we're supporting, the ones we call moderates,—who are these moderates?

Our Honor

One of the groups which we support is called Jaesh al-Islam. This is taken in the area of Damascus, and Jaesh al-Islam despises the Alawites. The Alawites are considered friends of Christians. They're much more moderate. And they [Jaesh] captured Alawite women, and they put them in steel cages—no privacy, no facilities, and they parade them around town in cages. This is one of the groups that the United States supports, and the U.S. State Department refuses to call them extremist. I would call that pretty extreme.

But if you don't think that's extreme, here's another example. Russia and Syria insisted that Ansar al-Sham be labeled as terrorist. Secretary Kerry refused to do it, and on the 13th of May of this year, they committed the massacre at Al-Zahra. This is a photograph that they have admitted is valid, but they said that the housewives that you see on the floor, they were fighters. Look for some weapons. What fighters go into battle barefooted? What kind of fighters go into battle wearing housedresses? What kind of fighters have world geographic maps on the wall, so that they can teach their children geography?

After they murdered these women, they captured—now, the children watched as they murdered their mothers. These are American allies! These are the moderates we support. After the children had to watch their mothers slaughtered, they were doused with gasoline, lit on fire, and burned to death.

What's happened to our country? What has happened to our country?

Here's a very recent one. The United States backs a group called Al-Zinki—it's Nour al-Din al-Zinki. They give them all these crazy names to make it hard to keep up. The United States pays the entire al-Zinki force. It's about a thousand terrorists. This group of five, paid for out of your pocket, and yours and yours, went into a hospital. They captured this little Palestinian refugee boy, terrified—if you look closely, you'll see that there's still an IV hanging out of his arm. They took him out to a town square in a pickup truck, and you can see one of them has him by the hair. And that individual who had him by the hair took him, slammed him down, sliced his head off with a knife, waved it to the crowd—"*Allah Akbar! Allah Akbar!*" A little boy who was so terrified, so frightened, so frail, suffering from a blood disease. The United States supports these people. We pay his salary! Your tax money pays his salary! Your tax money pays the salary of that man whose hand is on the head of that boy, and then severed it seconds later!

EIRNS/Stuart Lewis

Senator Black (right) and Syrian Ambassador Ja'afari at the Sept. 10 Schiller Institute conference.

You won't hear about this in the mainstream media, but we also funnel TOW anti-tank missiles through these so-called moderate groups, knowing that they're going to Al-Qaeda, knowing that they're going to ISIS.

This is the Syrian ambassador, the UN Ambassador from Syria, Bashar Ja'afari, a magnificent, heroic man, who—[laughter] Mr. Ambassador. [applause] I have to tell you a small story about him. One of the things that we do when we're toppling nations, is we try to buy off ambassadors, and get them to turn on their nations. Ambassador Ja'afari was approached. He was given a blank check—I think, do you still have that check? But, in any event, he's a great man of honor and courage, and he said, no, I will *not* betray my people; I will not slaughter my people for money. [applause] And I am very proud to know the Ambassador.

Now, people ask me, they say, why are you so passionate about this? You don't have any Syrian relatives. You don't have any Middle Eastern relatives. Well, you know, I was a Marine, and I started at Parris Island as a private. We used to stand at night, and we'd sing the Marine Corps hymn, and we said that "I will fight for right and freedom, and *to keep our honor clean.* I'm proud to claim the title of United States Marine." *Our honor is disgraced.* Our honor has been laden with filth in Syria. There is nothing more vile than what we have done to the people of Syria that's resulted in 400,000 deaths, and I want to change, I want to bring peace there. I want the people to have self-determination. I

don't want a bunch of foreign nations coming down and saying, this is the puppet government we want to install. The people of Syria want Bashar al-Assad. They should have the person that they want.

Now finally, I'll tell you, this is a group of Christian school children. We took a picture with the Patriarch, and if you look at the faces, it'll help to explain the passion that I have. If the United States continues on its present course, if the United States succeeds in toppling the government of Syria, it will be replaced by Al-Qaeda. And within two years, all of those joyous, smiling young children that you see, will be dead. That's why I'm very deeply concerned, and I am *determined* that we will turn around American policy in Syria.

Finally, just a last photo of what happens when people like Al-Qaeda take over. Now this is ISIS. They both are progeny of Al-Qaeda. They captured these 19 Yazidi women, and they tried to force themselves on them, and the women refused have multiple sex with strangers. And they took them out, and seconds after this photo was taken, they took them one at a time, and they burned them to death publicly for refusing to have sex with these people. *What has America done? What have we become?*

We're better than this. I know the American people are better than this. But the American federal government is not. And we need to make sure that somehow we change the direction that we've taken. Thank you very much.

'The Mask Has Fallen, The Truth Is There'

Ambassador Bashar Ja'afari, Permanent Representative of the Mission of the Syrian Arab Republic to the United Nations, addressed the Sept. 10 Schiller Institute conference in New York. An edited transcript follows.

Dennis Speed: Our final speaker, to the surprise of many of you, is Ambassador Bashar Ja'afari, Permanent Representative of the Syrian Arab Republic to the United Nations. [applause]

Ambassador Ja'afari: Ladies and gentlemen, thank you so much for coming on this Saturday, a hot Saturday, humid Saturday, to listen to us. I know that sometimes politics is boring, would bore the listeners. However, the issue is very important. It's not only about Syria, but it is about all of us. It's about the U.S.A., it's about Syria, Iraq, the Middle East, the whole Middle East—the whole world! And we will try to elaborate a little bit by adding to what my distinguished colleague, the Hon. Senator Richard Black has just pointed out.

History has shown to us that lies are not and could not be eternal. We know for sure, nowadays, that many tragic episodes in history were based on lies, meaning they were baseless and without any foundation. I could share with you hundreds of examples about what I'm saying, all of them derived *from the UN itself*, from the United Nations, where I represent my country. We have indeed too much information to share with you. We

EIRNS/Stuart Lewis

Ambassador Bashar Ja'afari, Permanent Representative of the Syrian Arab Republic to the United Nations, speaking at the Schiller Institute conference on Sept. 10.

could speak about what's going on in the world in general, or just in Syria, in particular, for hours, if not for days, and you would be surprised, because you have never heard anything of this information I'm going to share with you.

It is a great honor for me to have the opportunity to address this august audience from this podium in St. Bartholomew's Church in Manhattan. I convey to you my sincere salutes, and best wishes, and I thank the Schiller Institute, and thank you *all*, for offering this great honor to me and to my colleagues.

We meet today while we all are recalling the tragedy of September 11. It was one of the most sad and grievous days in the whole history of the United States. It also was a harsh and difficult lesson to learn for all nations and governments, that terrorism recognizes no boundaries or identities, and therefore should not be justified, protected, or concealed. I'm saying this, because Senator Black somehow gave some hints about the Saudi links to the events of 9/11. And I will elaborate a little bit on this issue, later on. Fifteen of the nineteen terrorists who did the 9/11 attacks, were Saudis. They were not Syrians; they were not Iraqis; they were not Algerians. They were Saudis.

These same Saudis were formed by what is called, commonly speaking, Wahhabism, which comes from the name of the founder of this school of thought, Mo-

The renovated mosque of of Muhammad Abdul Wahhab in Old Diriyyah, Saudi Arabia. Abdul Wahhab invented the strange version of Islam we know as Wahhabism and signed a pact of mutual loyalty with the Saud family in 1744. The British backed the Saud family from no later than 1788.

hammad Abdul Wahhab (1703-1792). Abdul Wahhab appeared all of a sudden in the Hijaz, the old name of Saudi Arabia, which is a fake name actually. Saudi Arabia is a fake name of the country, because "Saudi" means al-Saudi, the family of Saud; so it's as if you were changing the name of your own country to be the United States of Obama. [laughter] So this family stole the name of the country and transformed this country to fit its radical agenda. That happened in the late 18th Century.

The funny part of the story is that this school of thought was facilitated, created, and endorsed by the British intelligence of that time. So the British intelligence facilitated the creation of this radical movement in Islam, on purpose of course,— you know the British, how they act. Nothing is for free. [laughter]

In 1802, the followers of this crazy guy moved toward Karbala in Iraq. In Karbala, they attacked the shrines of the Shi'a Muslims, and in Damascus in 1810 they tried to invade the city, but the Syrians stopped them and defeated them at the walls of the city. Then they re-treated and went back to where they came from.

I'm giving you this background to show you that this crazy movement is not a newcomer. It has been there for centuries, a couple of times protected by the British, then by the Americans. It is not because they like them, but it is because their craziness fits those foreign agendas.

Manipulation of Islam

Islam is not about Saudi Arabia. In Damascus, in the greatest mosque in Damascus, called the Umayyad Mosque, in the middle, in the heart of the mosque, which is also the biggest and greatest mosque in Syria,— we have the shrine of St. John the Baptist, inside the mosque. The tomb of St. John the Baptist is in the middle of the mosque, where Muslims as well as Christians visit the tomb, and say their prayers. Senator Black told you about the Mufti of Syria, this wonderful man. Could you believe that his main political adviser is a Christian? The Mufti's political adviser is a Christian. Only in Syria—*only* in Syria. This is why we are extremely proud of our secularism. We are proud of what we are, whether we are

The shrine and tomb of John the Baptist, known as Yahya in the Koran. It is in the Umayyad Mosque in Damascus and is visited by Christians and Muslims.

Muslims or Christians, but we are not ready to become as crazy as the Saudis are. And we don't share, at all, their concepts of religion.

By the way, what ISIL is doing, and all these fanatic groups operating in Syria and Iraq, those who are beheading the boys, and women, and girls,— they have inherited beheading people by sword from the Wahhabis! Till now, ladies and gentlemen, in Saudi Arabia, after the Friday prayers, they behead people in the public square! Till now! It is not only ISIL! In Saudi Arabia itself, every Friday after the prayer, they behead people, publicly, in the public square, but using swords! So the story is not new. ISIL is not a newcomer; ISIL has been there for centuries, represented by the Saudis. And this is why they are protecting them and defending them and sending them weapons and money.

Most of us in this world believed after that black day of 9/11, that there would be a united international stand against terrorism. We were all optimistic at that time, if you remember, that finally, we will get together to fight terrorists. And that all nations will fight together against terrorists, their supporters, their funders, and their inspirational leaders. Unfortunately, what happened next, was the invasion of Iraq. So if the Saudis attacked New York, the Twin Towers, why go after Iraq, if the main reason was to avenge what happened in 9/11—and we all know, and we all knew at that time, that it was a Saudi conspiracy. Then why attack Iraq? Iraq is a secular country, like Syria. Syria, Iraq, and Algeria are the only three secular governments in the Arab world! Iraq is out the picture now; Iraq has become a hub of international terrorism, after the spreading of George Bush freedom over there. [laughter]

Algeria you know. Algeria was tested before us, in the early 1990s. They sent to them an early Arab spring, but it was defeated—thank God! So, only Syria remains. Only Syria remains; and Egypt, recently. And Egypt recently after the eviction of Morsi, who belongs to the same family of the radical movement of Islam. It is not about Islam; it is about radical movements, *pretending, claiming, alleging* that they represent Islam, but they don't.

Islam has become a good business for manipulation. Very good business for manipulation, *very* good business. Everybody makes business out of Islam very cheaply, and we will try to explain why. It's not about

Saudi Arabia TV

To this day, the Saudi government beheads those found guilty of adultery, apostasy, or sorcery. Here, a Saudi television screenshot of a public beheading in 2013.

politics. You are fed up with politics; I am also fed up with politics. It is about *geo*-political dimensions, rivalries, competition, dominance.

Then we said, what happened next unfortunately was the invasion of Iraq, under the very same pretext of fighting terrorism. That was a funny part of the story: When George Bush invaded Iraq, he said that he was doing that to combat terrorism; and to get rid of the wrongly alleged weapons of mass destruction—again, another lie. You know it. You know it, and let me tell you this story. I'm an eyewitness: I work at the UN and I know what I'm talking about, because I was there—a story that none of you have seen in the mainstream media, as Senator Black said.

Bremer Does the Dirty Work

After the invasion of Iraq, the United Nations, under the pressure of Tony Blair and George Bush at that time, sent what we call an investigation commission, called UNSCOM, headed by a Swede, Hans Blix, a scientist, to find the weapons of mass destruction in Iraq. The purpose was to show to the so-called international community that the invasion of Iraq was based on facts! There are weapons of mass destruction in Iraq, and we've *got* to find them and show them to the international community!

So they formed this commission of investigation

and sent it to Iraq. Of course, when I say "commission," it's about hundreds of people all paid off using Iraqi government funds, the Iraqi assets frozen by the United Nations. Billions of dollars were spent on the activities of this commission, at the expense of the Iraqi people. This commission spent—how long? — from 2003 and even before, up to 2008; in 2008 it was about to close the file, because the lie had become too big to swallow.

So they gathered the Security Council and asked the commission to submit its final report. But the funny part of this story is that this final report doesn't include any hint that Iraq *had* weapons of mass destruction. But the commission wouldn't be able to say that "Sorry Gentlemen, members of the Security Council, we haven't found anything in Iraq." That would run against the mainstream

U.S. Air Force/SSgt. D. Myles Cullen

"Iraq has become a hub of international terrorism, after the spreading of George Bush freedom over there." Here, U.S. Ambassador Paul Bremer (center) in Baghdad in 2004, who can take much of the credit for building ISIL.

propaganda spread by George Bush and Tony Blair at that time.

So everybody was cornered in the Security Council: They need to shut down the file! Because it had become too costly, and it is time to put an end to all this story. What to do?

They gathered a meeting of the Security Council—at midnight. Midnight. There was nobody, except the fifteen members of the Security Council. In a few minutes, the president gavelled the meeting to order, and said, "We endorse the report of the commission"—without saying anything—whether they found something or didn't find something. The issue is dead.

Now: What to do with the archives of the commission? The archives, a big scandal. The Council decided—ladies and gentlemen, listen to me carefully—to put the entire archives in iron cages, fire resistant, with locks, digital locks for which only the Secretary General knows the code. That was Number 1. Number 2: These locked cages will not be reopened until 60 years from now. [Audience groans.] I'm sure you haven't heard this story. Nobody will tell you this story. This is what happened. This is how they killed the investigation about why Iraq was invaded! And now,

none of us in this room will be able to wait 60 years to disclose that *a big lie* took place at that time. It will be too late to bring those responsible, accountable, to justice. There will be no George Bush; there will be no Tony Blair.

There will be three million Iraqis killed; one million Iraqi widows; *millions* of Iraqis without fathers; millions of Iraqi refugees in the world. And the whole of Iraq is destroyed!

And, *hundreds of billions of dollars*—the Iraqi assets overseas—have gone. Evaporated. Like the $800 million of Libya. Nobody knows where this money is. The *$800 million*—this is Libya alone.

The result of the invasion of Iraq was the killing of millions of civilians as I said, destroying the infrastructure, and having a failed state there. And more important, transforming Iraq into a hub of international jihadist terrorism.

I am saying this because all of the so-called ISIL, all of them, grew up in the American jails in Iraq. All of them. They were taken care of by the American soldiers in Iraq: So they knew them, how dangerous they are, and they didn't deal with them accordingly. Why? Because Mr. Bremer was insisting on dividing Iraq on a confessional, sectarian, religious basis. The Iraqis lived side by side for thousands of years, until Mr. Bremer came, and found out that they shouldn't continue like this. We've got to divide the country, we've got to give a part to the Sunni, then a part to the Shi'a, then a part to the Kurds, another part to the Assyrians, and so on. Doesn't that amount to saying the Iraqis were duped and stupid for living side by side for thousands of years before Bremer came?

Today, and after six years, my country, Syria, is still suffering from the fiercest terrorist war in the modern history of humanity. This unprecedented barbarian war reflects the bitter fact that terrorism is still being privileged with safe havens, money resources, some well-known government support, and the growth of terrorist ideologies and shelters around the world. Why do I say this? Because it wouldn't be that easy for a terrorist to leave Sydney, Australia, to take a flight to,— to change the flight three times, get five visas—Thailand visa, Indonesian visas, a Cambodian visa, whatever—and then find himself at Istanbul airport in Turkey. Then, a group of people would come to welcome him upon his arrival, and escort him to the Turkish border with Syria. Then somebody would give him money and weapons, and facilitate his entry into Syria.

Criminals with One-Way Tickets

This is not a tourist! This is not a tourist: This is a terrorist *known* in advance by the Australian intelligence services, before he left!

Unfortunately, some governments are calculating that, you know, we have this garbage in our societies. Let us export them to Syria. Let us get rid of this garbage by sending them to Syria and Iraq, where they will kill Syrians, and, probably, they might be killed by the Syrians also. But finally, we will get rid of them, because they are a burden on our societies.

The problem started when these terrorists did kill Syrians and Iraqis, but some of them changed their minds and wanted to get back to Australia, Belgium, Paris, London, Germany, the U.S.A., Canada,— and that was a big problem, because the scenario was totally different. This garbage shouldn't get back, was the idea initially. But they started to get back. And the Western democracy isn't able to prevent them from doing so. So what was the solution? The solution is, the British Prime Minister, the Australian Prime Minister, the Belgian Prime Minister, the French President, decided to withdraw citizenship from these terrorists if they *dare* to come back.

What would that mean? That means, you know guys, continue killing the Syrians until you are killed. But don't ever think about getting back. And this is what's going on now in Syria. They cannot go back to where they came from, because they lost their rights to citizenship.

Figure out that these prime ministers I have enumerated did not say that if these terrorists get back, we will take them to court; they didn't say that. We will hold them responsible—no, they didn't say that. We will hold them accountable—they didn't say that. So they didn't say that these people are terrorists. They said, "If you get back, we will withdraw citizenship from you," meaning, "You are a good terrorist. As long as you continue to kill the Syrians, you are a good terrorist. But if you think about getting back to Paris, Brussels, Sydney, whatever—then you will become a bad terrorist."

Yesterday, while I was reading your invitation to this great event, many noble ideas stopped me, especially those about a better future for our nations, away from wars and conflict—particularly the words of Friedrich Schiller, the inspiration of the Schiller Institute, and I quote him: "Born for that which is better."

Unfortunately, again, what is happening up to today in my country, Syria, goes totally against these great human principles. The Syrian people suffer, until this moment, from terrorism which is supported by regimes of well-known countries, such as Qatar, Turkey, France, and Saudi Arabia's Wahhabi family. I don't need to remind you here of the basic role of the Saudi family in supporting and funding the terrorists who committed the brutal crime of 9/11, as I said at the beginning. But do not forget the dangerous role of their pre-historic religious clerics who still inspire terrorists with ideas of jihad and hatred of other religions and ethnicities, all around the world.

Another story—I'm a storyteller. I was the ambassador of my country to Indonesia, the biggest Islamic country in the world—235 million Muslims in one country. But this country is composed of 17,000 islands; this is why we call it the Malay Archipelago. It's not an island, it's an archipelago, a huge number of islands.

I told Senator Black this story in one of our meetings. When I first arrived in Jakarta, I was surprised that every Friday, after the prayer, thousands of young girls and young women gathered in front of the Saudi Embassy in Jakarta. I asked the Saudi Ambassador, "What's going on, Ambassador? Why are these people gathered in front of your embassy?"

Sacred Principles

He said, "You know, Ambassador, these people are giving me a serious headache every Friday. They gather all these women who are carrying a baby and chanting slogans, asking for their rights in their local language," something that I couldn't understand at that time.

But all these women happened to fall victim in this way: There are Saudi businesspeople and Saudi religious clerics who come to Indonesia for business, for short periods of time,— they spend twenty days, up to one month maximum over there. So because they are *so* religious, they need to have sex with women in Indonesia. How can they do it? They go to the small villages in Indonesia, of very poor people—extremely poor people, but real, honest people; and they marry young girls, twelve years old or thirteen years old, and their dowry is only $100. So they give the father $100 and the father gives them his daughter, thinking that giving his daughter to somebody coming from the Holy Land of Islam, is itself a treasure.

The guy takes the girl for twenty days, two weeks, three weeks, whatever,— and then he divorces her before leaving, because he doesn't need her any more!

The girl finds herself pregnant. After nine months, she has a baby, but the baby doesn't have any father,— so no papers, no identity, and she cannot register the baby! Thousands of young Indonesian women find themselves in this situation every year!

I spoke to the Ambassador: "You should do something. This is bad for your image,— I mean, you cannot go on with this." He told me, "You know, Bashar, I have at the embassy a person called a religious attaché," meaning a guy in charge of religious matters, like the economic attaché, cultural attaché, military attaché,— they have this specific position called the "religious attaché." "And this religious attaché is stronger than me!" This is what he said. "I cannot do anything. I am the Ambassador, but I cannot do anything to stop this hemorrhage." That was in 1999.

And at that time, the Saudi regime used to spend $3 billion on educating Wahhabi Indonesian imams: $3 billion per year to educate Wahhabi Indonesian imams in the small villages. This is why, unfortunately, nowadays, in Southeast Asia we now have the same ISIL we have in the Middle East,— they have it over there. They did the Bali explosion if you remember, and the series of explosions at the five-star hotels in Jakarta. This is what the Saudis are.

I am Muslim myself, I am proud to be a Muslim, but I have nothing to do with this garbage. Nothing.

We have hopes for the legislation which passed yesterday in the House of Representatives and had already passed in the Senate, allowing the families of 9/11 victims to *sue* the Royal family—Royal, of Saudi Arabia, [laughter] in the U.S. courts. You know this Royal family, and what they are doing in the hotels in California and New York.

We hope that will pose a new course in U.S. foreign policy regarding fighting international terrorism and holding people responsible. Moreover, this terrorist war against Syria is accompanied by policies of Western states—led by the United States administration and Britain—based on violating international law and the Charter of the United Nations, disrespecting the sovereignty of the country, and acting against the *will* and interests of the Syrian people.

Senator Black elaborated on this issue, but I would like to add the following: That since the beginning of the Syrian crisis, in 2011, the Security Council endorsed and adopted sixteen resolutions on Syria. Now we have sixteen resolutions adopted by the Security Council on Syria. All of these resolutions start with the following in the Preamble paragraph: "The Security Council reiterates the confirmation of Syrian sovereignty, the territorial integrity of Syria, the political independence of Syria, the principle of non-interference in the domestic affairs of Syria . . ." All of these beautiful Tom and Jerry expressions are in the first paragraph of *each* resolution! And who violates these principles, sacrosanct principles,— the same ones who endorse the resolutions! The same influential people in the Security Council are the ones who are violating these beautiful wordings.

A UN Investigation

Another story. I always tell stories in my meetings, so one day in Geneva, when I was heading the Syrian government delegation to the intra-Syrian talks with Staffan de Mistura, the UN Secretary General's special envoy for Syria, he called me a storyteller. So the story is the following, and this is a very, very important one.

I will tell you this story chronologically, beginning in October 2012, so you will understand the message. The first attack in Syria using toxic gas took place five months later in Khan al-Assal, a small town in the sub-

UN/Jean-Marc Ferré

Ambassador Ja'afari (left) with UN Special Envoy to Syria Staffan de Mistura, during the intra-Syrian talks in Geneva, January 2016.

urbs of Aleppo, in March 2013. But in October 2012, some of what are called, commonly speaking, "Syrian opposition activists," formed and established, in Turkey, an office they called the "Office of Documentation on the Use of Chemical Weapons in Syria." They established this office *five months* before *anything* related to the issue of chemical weapons had happened in Syria. And all of a sudden, the Organization for the Prohibition of Chemical Weapons (OPCW), which is based in The Hague, in the Netherlands, gave this non-governmental center consultative status, meaning it endorsed the center as an OPCW consultative body on chemical issues.

We didn't understand why did it did that, because we didn't expect that something would happen *five months later*. Then in March 2013, they attacked Khan al-Assal in Aleppo, using chemical gas, and they killed 18 Syrian soldiers. Of course, CNN wouldn't speak about it. But 18 Syrian soldiers died of suffocation in this attack.

Immediately Al Jazeera, the Qatari channel, started spreading rumors that the Syrian army used chemical weapons. So the Syrian army used chemical weapons against itself. The Syrian army killed 18 officers and soldiers of its own troops!

Simultaneously, a series of similar attacks took place in Syria. I have the names; you are not familiar with the names, so I will not get into these details. Carla da Ponte, the Italian lady who was a member of the In-

dependent Investigation Committee of the United Nations on Syria, said that the armed groups of the opposition were the ones who used the chemical weapons in the attack against the town of Khan al-Assal in Aleppo. An Italian lady said that; she was immediately fired.

Then we come to the story of the Red Line, President Obama's Red Line. Because again, after this attack on Khan al-Assal, I got instructions the same day the attack took place— the same day, eight hours after the incident took place—I went myself to the office of the UN Secretary General Ban Ki-moon. I asked him to help the Syrian government in (a) verifying whether or not chemical weapons were used in Khan al-Assal and (b) identifying the perpetrators. This is what I myself asked Ban Ki-moon that day.

The guy was very nice, as you know. He asked me to give him some time to consult with the good guys on the Security Council. So he consulted with the good guys and he came back, two or three hours later, to tell me the following: "Mr. Ambassador, tell your government that I will assist your country with a verification to prove whether chemical weapons were used or not in Aleppo. But I'm sorry, I cannot assist you in identifying the perpetrators."

From Day One, they *knew* who did it! But they didn't want to reveal the identity of perpetrators.

We said, "Yes, you know what, Mr. Secretary General, help us in verifying if chemical weapons were used or not." It took him four months and eleven days to send us an investigation team, headed by a well known Swedish scientist, Dr. Ake Sellström. It took him and the Security Council *four months and eleven days*, to send a team to investigate whether chemical weapons were used in Aleppo. You know that with this kind of weapon, the traces evaporate. You cannot trace them after a couple of days; they are not there.

Obama's Red Line

More importantly, after four months and eleven days, Dr. Sellstrom arrived in Damascus on August 18 and President Obama made his speech and drew the "Red Line"—that was what Obama did his speech on

UN/J.C. McIlwaine

Ambassador Ja'afari addresses the UN Security Council, Aug. 22, 2016. At meetings of the Security Council "there are usually between 50 and 100 reporters ... when I take the floor, 50 of them disappear instantly! Because they don't want *to hear."*

August 20. Dr. Sellstrom was in Damascus at that time, on his way to Aleppo to investigate what happened in Khan al-Assal. He was still at the door of the hotel in Damascus, getting into his car. All of a sudden, we hear that another chemical attack took place in the suburbs of Damascus. All of a sudden, coincidentally, another attack took place in the suburbs of Damascus! That was done to shift the attention from Khan al-Assal to another place, because initially, they didn't want anybody to investigate what happened in Khan al-Assal. So the best way to do it, was to shift the focus, to create another spot of attention somewhere else!

And who did it? Read the French anchors, Christian Chesnot and Georges Malbrunot, who published an important book in 2014 that covers this matter, *The Roads to Damascus: The black file of Franco-Syrian relations*, which shows how the Elysée manipulated chemical weapons reports. In this book, they state that the French Minister for Foreign Affairs, Laurent Fabius, was behind this attack. It is a French book—but CNN will never speak about it, will never say anything about it. You will never hear anything about these issues in the mainstream media, because that would corroborate the accuracy of our statements.

Then,— isn't it paradoxical that Obama gives his warning and draws his Red Line on the 20th of August, and then, coincidentally, the chemical attacks in the suburbs of Damascus take place one day after, on the 21st? As if somebody is trying to say, "You know, Mr. President, they crossed the line. Go and punish them! Go and kill President Assad! The way your predecessor killed Saddam Hussein!" Isn't it funny? Would the Syrian government use chemical weapons while Dr. Sellström is in Damascus? I mean....

I'm sorry, maybe I have spoken too long. I will sum up. I told you I could speak for hours about ... [laughter, applause]. I'm really grateful to all of you for giving me this opportunity to share with you some insights from inside, something that you have never heard about. I try my best, as ambassador of my country, to share this information with the media accredited to the United Nations. But you know what? Every time I take the floor next to the Security Council, where there are usually between 50 and 100 reporters accredited from all over the world to the UN as reporters and journalists; when I take the floor, 50 of them disappear instantly! [laughter] Because they don't *want* to hear, because they know what I would say; they don't want to report it. The point for them is, by listening they would somehow be obligated to report,— so the best way to avoid reporting is by boycotting, by not being there.

I am saying this because too many people, too many ambassadors to the United Nations, come to me and say, "You know, Bashar, you are right. Your government is right. We know the truth, but we cannot say it. You can—God bless you—but we cannot say it." So the mask has fallen. The truth is there. If you dig a little bit, you will find scandals that take place at this United Nations—scandals. It's not a place to maintain peace and security, it is a place to *demolish* peace and security, to destabilize societies. It's very easy, *very* easy at the United Nations, to destroy a country.

I thank you very much. I still have too many things left to say, but out of respect for the audience, I thank you very much. [applause]

Once more, allow me to thank the LaRouche foundation also, my old friends in New York. They are doing great, actually. And the Schiller Institute, of course, and this beautiful audience. I'm grateful to you. God bless you.

Every Day Counts In Today's Showdown To Save Civilization

That's why you need EIR's **Daily Alert Service**, a strategic overview compiled with the input of Lyndon LaRouche, and delivered to your email 5 days a week.

For example: On Jan. 7, EIR's Daily Alert featured the British hand behind the pattern of global provocations toward war. Of special note is British Intelligence's role in instigating the Saudi Kingdom's attempt to set off a Sunni-Shia war. This religious war has been the intent of British strategy since the Blair-Bush attack on Iraq in 2003.

We also uniquely update you regularly on the progress toward the release of the suppressed 28 pages of the Congressional Inquiry on 9/11, which would expose the Saudi role.

Every edition highlights the reality of the impending financial crash/bail-in policies that would realize the British goal of mass depopulation.

This is intelligence you need to act on, if we are going to survive as a nation and a species. Can you really afford to be without it?

THURSDAY, JANUARY 7, 2016

Volume 2, Number 97

EIR Daily Alert Service

P.O. Box 17390, Washington, DC 20041-0390

- British Crown Pushing War and Genocide in 2016
- Financial Mudslide Goes On; Monetarist Tyranny Gloats over Bail-Ins
- Moody's Downgrades Portugal's Novo Banco
- Puerto Rico's Default: It's Every Vulture for Himself
- Wide Glass-Steagall Debate Set Off Again by Sanders Speech
- MI6 Mouthpiece Evans-Pritchard Touts Persian Gulf Chaos
- North Korea Tests a Miniaturized Hydrogen Bomb
- Uighur Terrorists Found in Indonesia
- Foreign Investors Are Flocking In to China

EDITORIAL

British Crown Pushing War and Genocide in 2016

IV. Western Europe and the Land-Bridge

Make German Railways Fit for the Silk Road

by Dean Andromidas

Sept. 13—Is German transport infrastructure fit for integration into the New Silk Road transport corridors now emerging throughout Eurasia? The New Silk Road is already there—it is a work in progress, and it is already integrating the entire Eurasian land mass from Spain and Portugal to Vladivostok and Shanghai. New Silk Road express cargo trains are now coming to German cities such Duisburg and Hamburg—and through Germany to France and Spain. But much work is yet to be done. While there are rail connections throughout the growing network, not all are optimized for efficient and high-speed transport of goods. Speeds average a sedate 60 kilometers an hour (37 miles per hour), and there are bottlenecks throughout the transcontinental network: An "express" train from China takes more than two weeks to arrive in many West European cities. Nonetheless, the technology exists to cut that time in half.

This report addresses one of those bottlenecks that lies in Germany and advances a solution to the problem that has been put forward by German engineers and citizens who possess the vision required for the 21st Century.

German engineers and regional citizens' initiatives have proposed a mega-project to facilitate the passage of high-speed cargo trains through the rail corridor along the Rhine valley between Bonn and Wiesbaden. Dubbed the Westerwald-Taunus Tunnel (WTT), it entails building an 118-kilometer tunnel from Saint Augustine (Sankt Augustin), near Bonn on the east bank of the Rhine, to Hochheim near Wiesbaden, at the

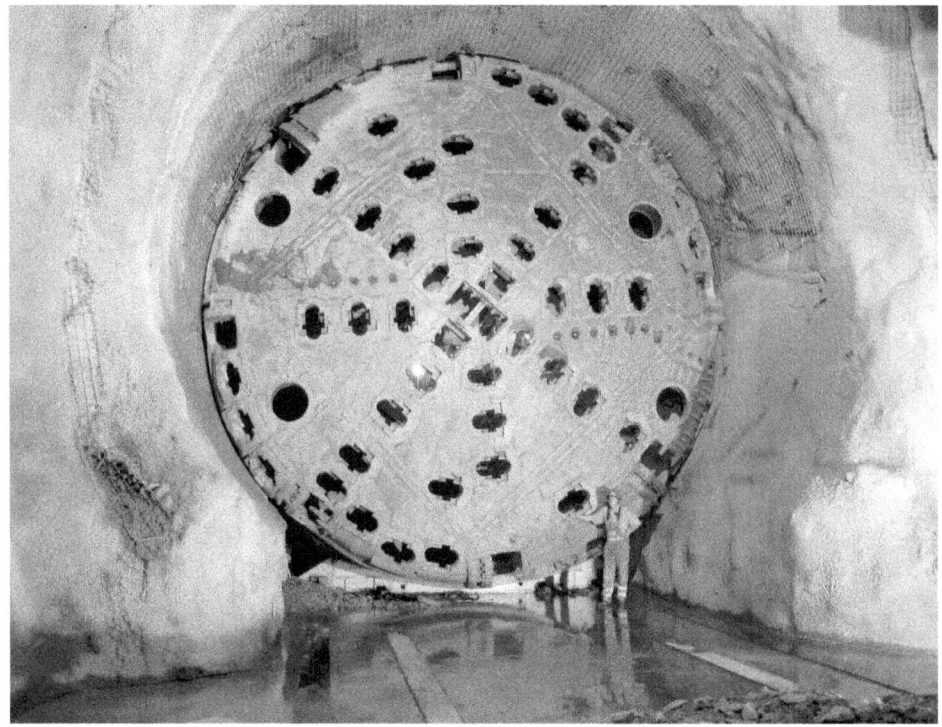

The head of an S-210 Tunnel Boring Machine used to excavate the Gotthard Base Tunnel under the Swiss Alps, shown after "breakthrough." Four such machines were used. The chisels have already been removed. The diameter is 8.8 meters (29 feet); the length of the machine is 400 meters (1,312 feet).

junction of the Main and Rhine rivers. It will be 50 kilometers shorter than the existing 170-kilometer route through the Rhine valley. Modeled after the newly completed Gotthard Base Tunnel under the Swiss Alps, it will have double tracks passing through each of twin tunnels, allowing cargo trains to travel at speeds up to 160 kilometers an hour (100 miles per hour), possibly unmanned.

The WTT will bypass one of the narrowest and deepest stretches of the Rhine Valley, especially between Bingen and Bonn. While this region is the most picturesque part of the Rhine Valley and has UNESCO World Heritage status, it has perhaps the most antiquated rail infrastructure in Germany. This stretch of railway is more than 150 years old and was designed for trains with an axle weight of 3 tons, not the current 23 tons, which has caused sections of the line to sink. Yet this is the primary route for cargo trains. No less than 400 freight trains pass through the valley every 24 hours. While Deutsche Bahn, the German national rail company, has built a high-speed passenger line through this region, it does not carry cargo trains.

The proposed WTT is a crucial link in the emerging New Silk Road that integrates Eurasia. Moreover, the project could serve as a paradigmatic solution for the dramatic expansion of rail freight throughout Europe.

Trans-European Transport Network

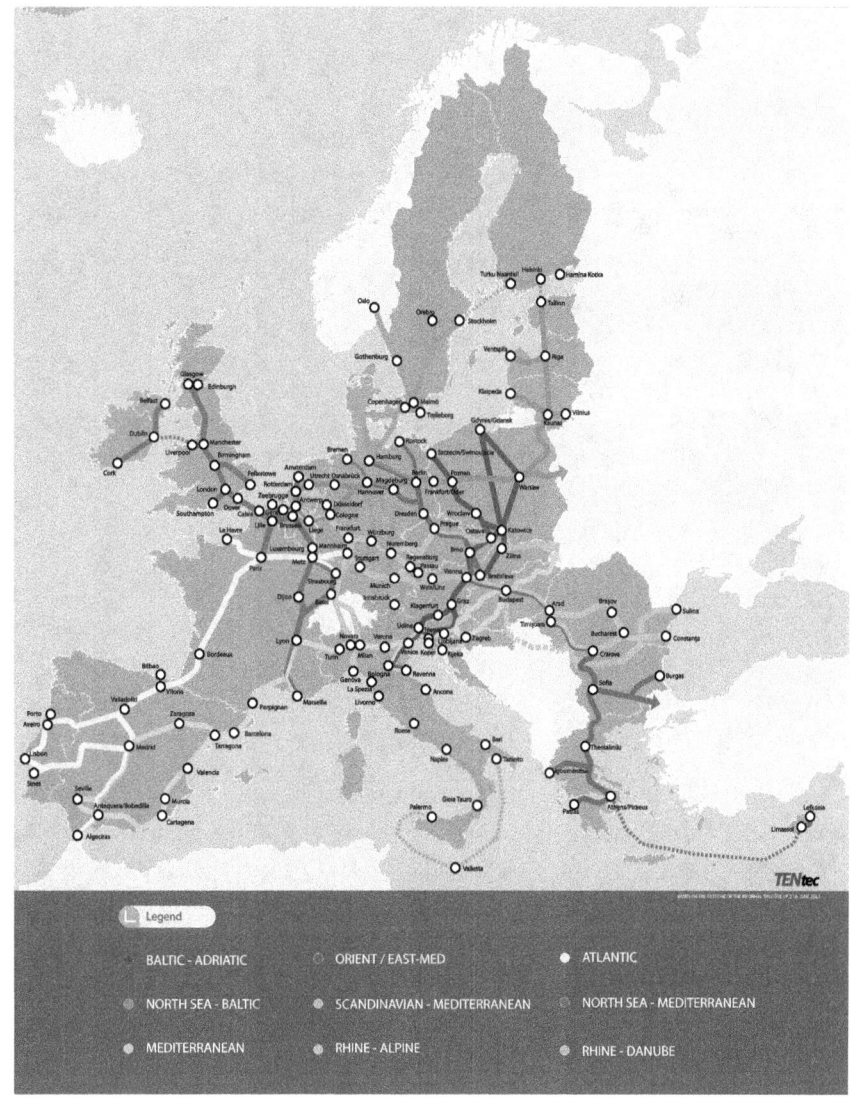

European Commission

The Bottleneck of All Bottlenecks

Cargo trains are already traveling from Central China to West European cities, including Lodz, Poland; Duisburg and Hamburg in Germany; Lyon in France; and cities in Spain, Switzerland, and other countries. Most of these trains take one of two routes. One route begins in Chengdu, the capital of Sichuan province in Central China, where it interconnects with the Chinese network. Traveling west from Chengdu, it goes through Kazakstan and across Russia, through Moscow to Brest in Belarus, and on to Lodz, Poland, and then continues west into Germany. A second route begins at Dalian on the Yellow Sea in northern China, where cargoes from South Korea and Japan can be loaded, enters Russia at Zabaikalsk, goes across Siberia to Moscow and then on to Lodz.

At Lodz, in the center of Poland, the trains enter the Trans-European Transport Network of corridors. These corridors were defined more than two decades ago with the aim of developing an efficient intermodal transport network linking Europe's major ports with the interior of the continent. Now they must also serve to link Europe with the New Silk Road. For example, from Lodz, the Chinese trains can travel south to the Adriatic

Rhine-Alpine Corridor

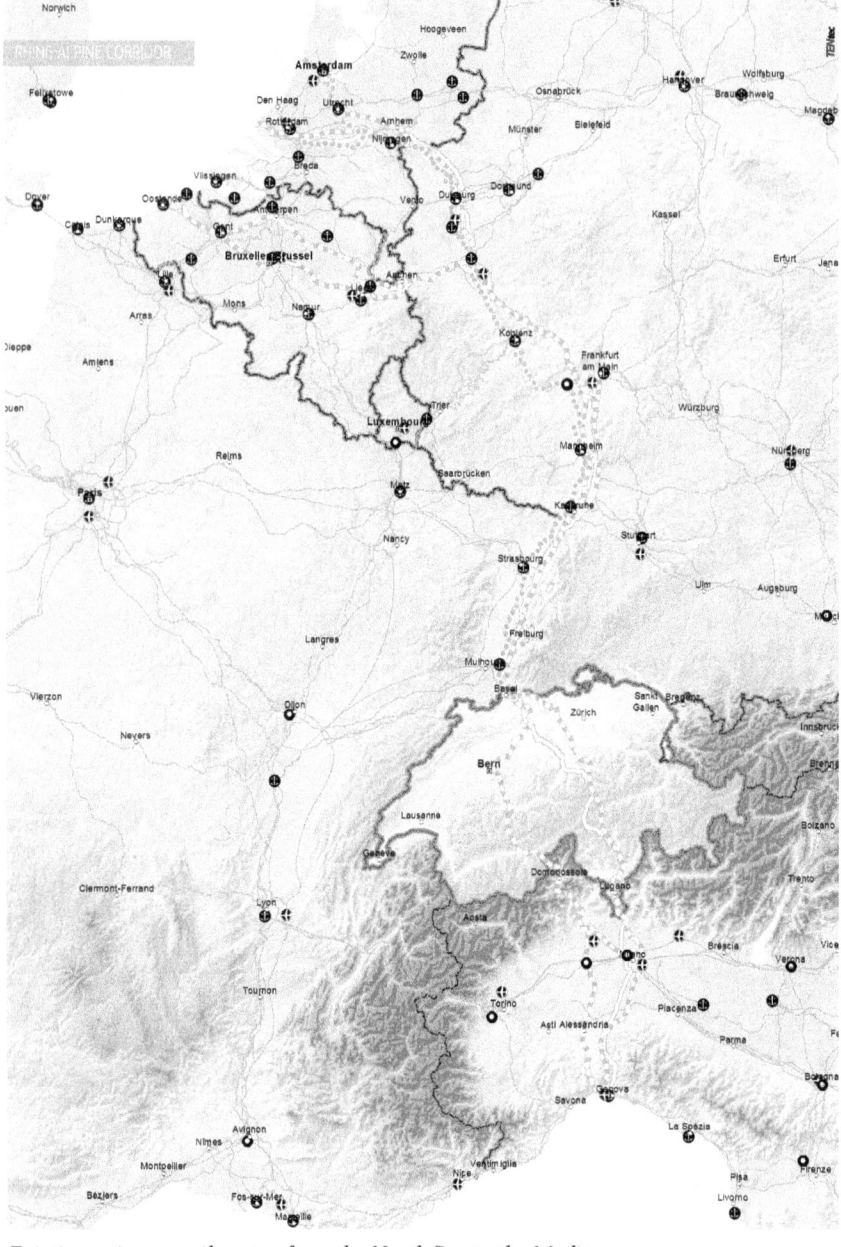

Existing primary rail routes from the North Sea to the Mediterranean.

terminates at Duisburg, which lies on the latter corridor.

The Rhine-Alpine corridor links the North Sea ports of Amsterdam, Rotterdam, Antwerp, and Zeebrugge with the Italian port of Genoa on the Mediterranean. Entering Germany near Oberhausen, the route heads south up the Rhine Valley all the way to Basel, where it divides. One branch goes through the new Gotthard Base Tunnel and the other through the Lötschberg Base Tunnel. These two tunnels under the Alps are new. Both lines continue south into Italy and terminate at Genoa.

Passing through one of the most densely populated regions in Europe and its industrial heartland, the Rhine-Alpine Corridor is the most traveled in Western Europe. This same corridor links into all the major East-West corridors of Europe and the North Sea-Mediterranean Corridor, which links Glasgow, Scotland and the French port of Marseille, and passes through the Channel Tunnel. The Rhine-Alpine Corridor also links into the Atlantic Corridor at Mannheim, Germany where it travels west to Paris and southwest through France and into Spain, where it branches off to the Portuguese ports of Porto, Aveiro, Lisbon and Sines and links to Spain's largest port, Algeciras, on the Bay of Gibraltar.

To go east, as mentioned, the Rhine-Alpine Corridor links into the North Sea-Baltic Corridor, through which trains pass to and from China and Russia. At Frankfurt and Mannheim, the Rhine-Alpine Corridor links into the Rhine-Danube Rail Freight Corridor, which reaches the Romanian port of Constantza on the Black Sea.

In Italy, it links into the Mediterranean Corridor that begins at Seville in the southwest of Spain and runs along the Mediterranean coast of Spain, France, and northern Italy; it continues eastward, passing through Budapest to reach the Ukrainian border.

Sea and the Mediterranean along the Baltic-Adriatic corridor, which runs from the Polish port of Gdansk on the Baltic through Eastern Europe and Vienna to Venice on the Adriatic.

Trains headed into Western Europe travel along the North Sea-Baltic Sea corridor, which connects Tallinn, Estonia on the Baltic with the North Sea ports of Bremen, Amsterdam, Rotterdam, and Antwerp. This corridor intersects the Rhine-Alpine Corridor. In this way, an express cargo train from Chengdu via Poland,

Thus all rail cargo coming from China and heading to points in western Germany, France, Spain, Portugal, Switzerland, and northwestern Italy must pass through this corridor. But the corridor is already tremendously overburdened by the huge volumes of cargo from the big North Sea ports of Rotterdam and Antwerp, respectively Europe's largest and second largest ports.

The Rhine-Alpine Corridor is the very backbone of the European rail freight network, yet its German segment is a serious bottleneck which the German government and Deutsche Bahn have so far refused to adequately address.

The New *Steel* Silk Road

The New Silk Road has to become a new, high-tech steel road employing the most advanced railway technology and operating on a separate, cargo-dedicated rail network capable of carrying cargo trains at speeds above 160 kilometers per hour.

Transcontinental railways are often seen as the alternative to shipment by sea, but a closer look reveals that they can become a serious competitor to air freight. While cargo trains carry 120 containers on average, the latest container ships carry up to 18,000. There could never be enough capacity to carry this trade on rails. Nonetheless, railways do compete with ships when shipping to points in the interior of Eurasia—for example, between Germany and points in Central Asia, western China, and western Siberia.

In densely populated regions such as Western and Central Europe, railways must provide an attractive alternative to truck transport to improve efficiency. The railways must also work hand in hand with overseas shipping as part of the intermodal transportation system that will efficiently move cargos from Eurasia's peripheral ports to points in the interior.

Reducing current travel times of two weeks or more from Chengdu or Dalian to one week or less at lower costs, would make railways competitive with air freight. But the issue is not just transporting laptops from China to the European market, but developing the huge underdeveloped regions along these transcontinental corridors. Such development requires machinery and technical equipment. To enable Western European manufacturers to respond to this need, a separate cargo network is required, which will enable the full development of freight-specific technologies, without having to make the compromises involved in using a single network for freight and passenger traffic. For example, on a separate network, freight trains could be run automatically without drivers. And a separate network would increase freight capacity. Eventually, magnetically levitated train systems will be used for cargo.

To consider the requirements of such a freight-specific network across Eurasia is a task for several reports. Nonetheless, the example of the Rhine-Alpine Corridor, and the WTT within it, illuminates several key issues.

The creation of cargo-dedicated rail lines has begun in Europe. Both France and Spain have built cargo-dedicated lines along the Atlantic Corridor, and other countries such as Belgium and Hungary are considering doing the same. On the Rhine-Alpine Corridor, the Netherlands is the most advanced with its cargo-dedicated Betuweroute, which runs from the Port of Rotterdam to the German border at Zevenaar-Emmerich. It was begun in 1997 and opened in 2007. Built at a cost of 4.7 billion euros, the 160-kilometer line includes 18 kilometers of tunnels and has 130 bridges and viaducts totaling 12 kilometers. It is designed to carry trains with an axle weight of 23 tons at a speed of 120 kilometers an hour. Experiments will begin soon to test automatic trains without drivers.

While it carries more than ten percent of the cargo volume arriving in Rotterdam, its throughput is being hindered because Germany, despite agreements, has yet to expand transport capacity from the German border at Emmerich, and throughout the rest of the Rhine-Alpine Corridor in Germany.

Belgium would also like to build a freight-dedicated line from Antwerp, Europe's second largest port, to Mönchengladbach on the German border along the route of the old Iron Rhine Railway, which was closed down in the 1990s.

From the other end of the corridor, Switzerland has become a heavy lifter in rail projects. With the aim of getting trucks off of the nation's highways, it has constructed two railway tunnels that are among the longest in the world. While these are dual use—freight and passenger trains—they have increased the efficiency of the system dramatically. The first is the Lötschberg Base Tunnel through the Bernese Alps, built below the old mountain tunnel. The 35-kilometer tunnel has two single-track tubes. While one tube is finished and has been in operation since 2007, the second tube has not been fully completed because funds had to be transferred to the second huge tunnel project, the Gotthard Base Tunnel under the St. Gotthard Pass.

The Gotthard Base Tunnel, after 20 years of construction and the excavation of 28 *million* tons of rock, was officially opened in June of this year; regularly scheduled service will commence in December. At 57 kilometers (35.4 miles), it is the longest and deepest rail tunnel in the world and an inspiration for infrastructure planners throughout the world.

Where the Vision Ends

This visionary approach ends at the German border. Under the "schwarze Null" (black zero) budget policy of German Finance Minister Wolfgang Schäuble, "vision" has been banned from policy making. After almost a decade of pressure from Dutch interests in the Rhine-Alpine Corridor, Germany has finally relented, but has taken the cheapest and least desirable option. Rather than building a dedicated, double-track freight line along the entire length of the corridor, it has only committed itself to building a third track along the existing passenger line that will go from Emmerich to Oberhausen, a distance of 73 kilometers. While the third track will be dedicated to freight, it will not permit high speed and will hardly solve the problem along the Rhine Valley. Work is to begin this year and is scheduled to be finished in 2025, at the cost of 1.5 billion euros. But don't hold your breath.

Germany took a similar approach in the Upper Rhine Valley for the Mannheim-Karlsruhe-Basel line, where the plan has been to simply upgrade the line and lay two more parallel tracks along certain sections to support high-speed trains. Begun in the 1980s, it was expected to be finished by 2008, but still remains unfinished with no date set for completion, although the German government "hopes" it could be completed by 2030. And this stretch of the Rhine Valley does not present great topographical challenges, since the valley is broad and relatively flat. One of its primary functions is to serve as the approach from Germany to the new Gotthard Base Tunnel. Although this

Westerwald-Taunus Tunnel

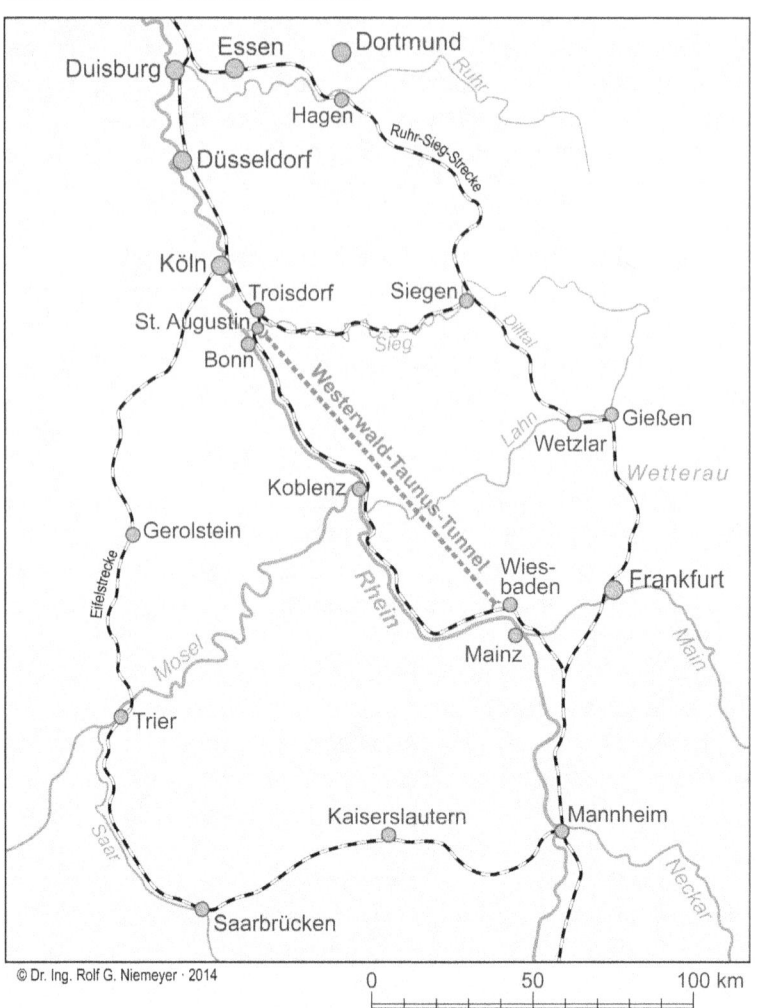

© Dr. Ing. Rolf G. Niemeyer · 2014

is one of the most important sections of the Rhine-Alpine Corridor, the upgrade is primarily for passenger trains.

Build the WTT, Establish a New Paradigm

By implementing the principle that the future of rail cargo operations must entail the establishment of an entirely new, independent rail freight network, the WTT could be the game changer that launches a new paradigm for rail transportation in Germany and the new Steel Silk Road.

The registration for the WTT project, inspired by the Gotthard Base Tunnel and drafted by Dr.-Ing. Rolf G. Niemeyer, is available on the website www.westerwald-taunus-tunnel.de/ It indicates that all of the technology and engineering know-how required for the project has been proven and is readily available. The

The Westerwald-Taunus Tunnel is proposed as an alternative to the present route on the bank of the Rhine River, shown here as it passes Burg Katz. The present rail infrastructure is more than 150 years old and has a limited load-bearing capacity for the 400 freight trains which pass through this section daily.

The tunnel must cut through the Rhenish Massif (*Rheinisches Schiefergebirge*), the geological formation that includes the Westerwald and Taunus ranges, and will use the Gotthard Base Tunnel configuration—two tracks passing through each of two parallel tunnels, with connecting tunnels between the two for emergencies and maintenance operations. The tunnel will be in two segments, one under the Westerwald and the other under the Taunus range. Eight boring machines similar to the ones used on the Gotthard Base Tunnel could operate simultaneously, working from both directions on each parallel pair of tunnels in each segment. Assuming a construction cost of 45 million euros per kilometer (2012 estimate), the tunnel alone will cost an estimated 5.3 billion. Adding the rail lines, technical equipment, and signaling system, the estimated total cost is 10 billion euros.

The current traffic through the Rhine Valley is 400 freight trains per day, and the tunnel will enable a large increase. Modern signaling technology is so good that it will permit more trains per day (720 per track, 1440 per day) than is practically feasible given other constraints.

The projected cost of the WTT compares with the 177-kilometer Cologne-Frankfurt high-speed rail line, begun in 1995 and finished in 2002, which parallels Germany's A3 Autobahn and cost 6 billion euros.

Too expensive? The promoters compare the cost to the "rescue" of German banks, pointing out that the rescue of WestLB, the German Landesbank, cost taxpayers 18 billion euros, while the rescue of IKB Deutsche Industriebank, HRE-Hypo-Real East, and others cost a total of 74 billion euros. They might have added the European bank bailout that was camouflaged as the Greek bailout, which cost more than 250 billion euros.

Using tunnels for a rail freight network would be very attractive along other sections of the corridor that pass through high-density population centers, both for safety and to permit high speed. It is about time that a few railway tunnels were built to improve a rail network that is, in part, more than 150 years old.

tunnel will traverse a straight line beginning at the town of St. Augustine, east of Bonn and not far from the two railway marshalling yards at Cologne. It will terminate at Hochheim near Wiesbaden, where it can connect with the rail line leading to the nearby Mainz-Bischofsheim marshalling yard. From there, various rail lines go south along the Rhine-Alpine Corridor, and there are also connections to lines going east and west. The route will be 50 kilometers shorter than the old 150-kilometer Rhine Valley route.

An alternative is to have the line terminate near Wiesbaden-Schierstein on the other side of Wiesbaden, where it could link with the line to Mainz-Bischofsheim from further down the Rhine. The former configuration would be 118 kilometers long and the latter, 107 kilometers.

The Silk Road Dynamic Opens Up New Opportunities for Germany

by Helga Zepp-LaRouche, chairwoman of the German political party,
Civil Rights Movement Solidarity (BüSo)

This editorial was written for the German newspaper Neue Solidarität *of Sept. 15.*

A strategic transformation has taken place in the past two weeks—although unnoticed or deliberately suppressed by the mass media in Germany—that at long last gives rise to the justifiable hope that positive solutions for the most serious problems of our time will be found. A series of summits in Vladivostok, Beijing, and Vientiane has brought about a complete reorientation of the relations among the majority of nations in the world. This new strategic situation gives us here in Germany both the opportunity and the challenge to productively achieve the economic and cultural potential of our country .

en/kremlin.ru

Russia President Vladimir Putin looks on as Japanese Prime Minister Shinzo Abe and President of the Republic of Korea Park Geun-hye greet each other on Sept. 3 at the Eastern Economic Forum plenary session.

At the Eastern Economic Forum in Vladivostok, on September 2-3, the integration of the Eurasian Economic Union and China's "One Belt, One Road" initiative was advanced. That is a huge step toward a potential common economic space from the Atlantic to the Pacific. Japanese Prime Minister Shinzo Abe spoke for the 3,000 participants of the conference in emphasizing the intention to develop the Russian Far East as an export hub for the entire Asia-Pacific region.

A very important secondary aspect of this conference was the progress that President Vladimir Putin and Prime Minister Abe were able to achieve with respect to the Russo-Japanese relationship, which is to be consolidated in December when Putin makes a state visit to Japan. They specifically discussed, among other issues, a peace treaty between the two nations. That enhances the environment for Germany to request that the next

U.S. President accept a peace treaty between the United States and Germany.

The G-20 Summit in Hangzhou on September 4-5, which China had carefully prepared for more than a year with many pre-conferences, signalled a complete realignment of relations among the countries of Asia and beyond—in stark contrast to what is being reported in the Western press. President Xi Jinping's intention to transform the G-20 Summit from an association dealing with crisis management, into an alliance that permanently guides the fate of humanity for the benefit of all, took a great step forward. As President Putin rightfully commented, the results of the G-20 summit are not legally binding, but they constitute a trend for the community of nations, and any state that is working against them will be noticed.

The new trend, established at Hangzhou, is for innovation as the basis of global economic growth, and

cc/Ryan Lim　　　　　　　　　　　　　　　cc/Elizabeth Cromwell

In the wake of the Vladivostok, G-20, and ASEAN Plus China conferences, Philippines President Rodrigo Duterte (left) announced Sept. 13 that he has cancelled the joint U.S.-Philippines patrols in the South China Sea, calling them needless provocations.

that means, above all, promoting the development of developing countries through their optimal participation in scientific advances. That is an aim of China, as reflected in the much larger number of developing countries invited to the G-20 summit as guests than ever before. Xi Jinping underscored China's commitment to realize the industrialization of Africa as a priority, and other government spokesmen welcomed increased investment in Africa by India and Japan. Given the longstanding problems, Xi has long called for the immediate implementation of a new global financial architecture that would serve an innovation-driven growth strategy and bring productivity to the highest possible level.

Asia Rebuffs Obama, Opts for New Silk Road

The ASEAN Plus China Summit, which followed the G-20, handed President Obama a devastating rebuff when he tried to show that "the United States makes the rules, and not China." The ASEAN nations did not support Obama's attempt to recognize as binding, the recently issued ruling of the International Court of Arbitration in The Hague on the territorial conflicts in the South China Sea. On the contrary, the ASEAN members supported China's position, that all future conflicts should be solved by friendly negotiations and diplomacy, as provided for in the United Nations Law of the Sea Convention of 1982. Even the Philippines, whose previous government had filed the case at The Hague, is

distancing itself from this ruling and has opted for peaceful dialogue with China.

And rather than endorsing the Trans-Pacific Partnership (TPP) free trade zone as demanded by Obama, they committed to collaborating with China in the Regional Comprehensive Economy Partnership (RECEP) and with the institutions of the Silk Road Economic Belt such as the Asian Infrastructure Investment Bank (AIIB), the New Development Bank (NDB), and the Silk Road Fund. And just in time for the Summit, Canada announced its membership in the AIIB, which Obama had wanted to prevent.

International media such as *Forbes* and *Time* magazine reported Obama's complete diplomatic isolation. In fact, the Asian nations rejected Obama's confrontation policy and made it unmistakably clear that they prefer China's proposal that they adopt the Chinese economic model and cooperate in the international projects of the New Silk Road.

As for Obama's "last option" for imposing the rules—through passage of the two U.S.-dominated free trade agreements, TPP and Trans-Atlantic Trade and Investment Partnership (TTIP)—it is gone: The leaders of the U.S. Senate and House of Representatives, Mitch McConnell and Paul Ryan, have meanwhile declared, for tactical electoral reasons, that these two proposals will no longer be on the legislative agenda this year, and both Hillary Clinton and Donald Trump have come out against them.

But that's not the only bad news for Obama: On Sept. 9, and thus immediately before the 15th anniversary of the attacks of September 11, 2001, the House of Representatives unanimously passed the Justice Against Sponsors of Terrorism Act (JASTA), which allows American citizens to sue Saudi Arabia for its role in the 9/11 attacks. It had already been passed in the Senate unanimously. Thus Obama, as *The Hill* stated, finds himself in a dilemma: whether to draw on himself the wrath of the 9/11 victims' families and many other Americans by a

September 16, 2016　**EIR**　　　　　　　　　　　　　　　　　　　　　　　　New Epoch　49 veto or a pocket veto, or to be investigated in the course of any judicial inquiry into Saudi Arabia's role because—in the best tradition of Bush and Cheney—he covered up this monstrous scandal throughout his entire presidency.

Germany Has New Options

What is the significance of this transformed strategic constellation, which includes optimism for a successful the ceasefire agreement in Syria and military cooperation between the United States and Russia, which has just been agreed to between Secretary of State John Kerry and Foreign Minister Sergey Lavrov, and which allows hope for an end to the war in Syria? Since the Russian intervention in Syria, and China's and India's diplomatic and economic engagement in Syria, there is also hope for economic reconstruction as part of the building of the New Silk Road in this region.

This dramatically changed strategic situation means that Germany has completely new political options—namely, to cooperate with China and the other Asian nations in the economic development of Southern Europe, the Mideast, and Africa, and by doing so, to seize the means to solve the refugee crisis—and at the same time, to dry out the breeding grounds for terrorism.

Italian Prime Minister Matteo Renzi has apparently recognized the signs of the times, as he presented precisely this perspective in an interview with the Chinese television network CCTV, saying that Italy—in the tradition of Marco Polo and Matteo Ricci—will collaborate comprehensively with China on the New Silk Road, not least in the development of Africa.

Against that backdrop, the speech of German Development Minister Gerd Müller in the most recent budget debate in the Bundestag was highly significant. He compared the horrendous situation in Africa with the impoverishment of broad sections of the population in the early phase of capitalism, and demanded a large-scale Marshall Plan for that continent and other developing countries. This is only possible if German, Italy, and the other European nations, together with China,

CCTV screen grab

Italian Prime Minister Matteo Renzi, in an interview with China's CCTV Sept. 3, announced that Italy will collaborate comprehensively with China on the New Silk Road, not least in the development of Africa.

India, Japan, and other countries develop the New Silk Road into the World Land-Bridge, as the BüSo has demanded for so long. Ms. Merkel's fortunes are sinking, the EU finds itself in a continuous process of dissolution after Brexit, and right-populist to right extremist parties are gaining strength in many European countries. None of this would be happening if the people of Europe could see a perspective for the future. The Alternative für Deutschland would not have beaten the CDU in Mecklenberg-Pomerania if Ms. Merkel had said: "We can do this, together with China and the nations of Asia; we can carry out a new Marshall Plan with the building of the New Silk Road into the Mideast and Africa." But we are saying that. We cannot lose this great historic opportunity to create a new and just world economic order, in the way we lost the great historic opportunity of 1989. At that time, Britain, the United States, and France forced the euro on us as the price for German reunification. Today even a fool can see that the euro is a failed experiment, with negative interest rates, laughable 0.3% growth in the Eurozone, and bankrupt banks all over Europe.

Today Britain is out, the United States is isolated, and France is economically finished. Germany could do them—and itself—the greatest favor by replacing the old "no longer sustainable model," as Xi Jinping called it, with a win-win perspective for the development of all. It is high time that Germany looked to its own interests.